Demystifying the Spanish Subjunctive.

Feel the fear and 'subjunctive' anyway.

Probably the most comprehensive Spanish Subjunctive workbook on the market.

Gordon Smith-Durán
Cynthia Smith-Durán

LightSpeed Spanish

2015

First Printing: 2015 Edition 2

ISBN 978-1512073027

LightSpeed Spanish
221 Calle Circular,
Las Dehesas,
Valdenuño Fernández,
Guadalajara,
España.
19185

www.lightspeedspanish.co.uk

Dedication

To the many beautiful people who have helped this book to come into being. A very special thanks goes to Michael Smith. Were it not for the conversation we had together one day in 2014 this book would never have been written. (Or at least not as quickly!)

Your help, please.

We are self publishing authors which means that we have to proof read our own books. No matter how much we check them, we, inevitably, end up with the occasional typo or error.

If you were to spot any glaring errors as you work through this book, please feel free to let us know at:

lightspeedspanish@hotmail.co.uk

or contact us through our website:

www.lightspeedspanish.co.uk

Acknowledgements

Quotation on p.36 taken from:

Butt, J, Benjamin, C. Grammar of Modern Spanish, 2004. London. p 248

Contents

Desmitificando el Subjuntivo español.
Demystifying the Spanish Subjunctive.

Donde empezó todo-Where this all began.

As I begin to write this book in 2015 I can look back on the many fascinating years that I have spent learning to understand, utilize and, to some smaller degree, dominate the Spanish language. It hasn't been an easy task, of that I must admit. However, in many respects this experience has been the one that has most fulfilled and altered the entire course of my life. (Para mejor, claro.)

If I were to consider all of the steps through which this process has taken me, facing the task of learning the Spanish subjunctive was the only one that truly struck fear into my very core. But, why? It may well have been because of its worryingly long name, or because I didn't know what the word 'subjunctive' meant, or maybe because my English language training at school had been so 'light' that I had been blissfully oblivious to the existence of the present and past subjunctive. (I doubt my English teacher was aware of them either.)

And yet, thanks to two lovely people, I have become very much aware of how we do use them in English, and of how they appear far more often than you might imagine. We'll come to the Imperfect, or what I prefer to call the Past Subjunctive later, and then I'll have the opportunity to talk about the other person who has guided me no end in understanding this tricky tense (my wife, Cynthia).

For the moment, however, let me show you how I learnt about the way the Present Subjunctive is used in English.

During an email conversation with my good friend Peter Løvstrøm, my eyes were opened to the vast number of sentences in English that take the Present Subjunctive. Before that, I hadn't really paid attention to these kind of word structures and was thus unaware of the fact that they were identical in format to the Spanish Present Subjunctive.

Here are a few examples that Peter offered me:

It is important that you **be** there.

(Rather than 'that you **are** there.')

It is necessary that he **do** it immediately.

(And not, 'that he **does** it.')

It is imperative that we **be** present at the meeting.

(Normally it would be, 'that we **are** present.')

It is advisable that she *have* some rest before the trip.

 (Instead of, 'that she **has** some rest.')

I demand that I *be* allowed to speak to my lawyer.

(The normal conjugation is, 'that I **am** allowed.')

The doctor insists that the patient *stay* in the hospital.

(Rather than, 'that the patient **stays**.')

Now, I have to say that much of this kind language is falling into disuse. Lots of people typically use the version that appears in brackets. Yet, as you read the above sentences, you probably noticed how natural they all seemed. That's because it's likely that, at some point, we've all heard them used.

As you can see, the system we use in English is to apply the verb in its infinitive (complete) form. This is our subjunctive. We don't make it agree with the person mentioned in the sentence. Now, for me, discovering that was a real eye opener.

Beforehand I had always attributed our fear of the Spanish Present Subjunctive to the fact that we didn't have it in English and thus we had no frame of reference for it. Wrong again! (I've lost track of how many times I've been wrong in my assumptions about things. Perhaps one day I'll get stuff right on a consistent basis...but I doubt it.)

Perhaps, had I known from the start that both the Present and the Past (Imperfect) Subjunctive existed in English, I wouldn't have been quite so nervous.

Llegando al Subjuntivo español.

Getting to the Spanish Subjunctive.

So, even though for a long time I was unaware of the Present Subjunctive in English, what was certain was that I was more than awakened to its existence in Spanish.

During my learning journey up to that point I had already heard the mantra that invariably comes from the more advanced students who, for whatever reason, feel that it's their duty to scare the pants off you.

They seemed to revel in offering me the foreboding warning of... "Wait until you get to the subjunctive. You're going to die!".

Thanks to all those dire warnings, not only was I scared of the Subjunctive but also I knew only too well that at some point I was going to have to face it head on. However, probably like many of you reading this book, I hoped that I could find a different way; some trick of language that would allow me to avoid it for as long as possible, if not forever.

The more I studied, however, the more I realised that avoiding the subjunctive in Spanish was akin to trying to speak Spanish without verbs, to talk without moving your mouth or to breathe underwater. It just wasn't happening. I was going to have to do it 'me gustara o no'. (Whether I liked it or not.)

Mis primeros pasos tentativos.

My first tentative steps.

Once I'd taken the decision to learn how this devilish tense worked, I'm proud to say that I did it with my usual exuberance; throwing myself into the fray, and buying every text book I could find that made reference to the subjunctive.

Then, surrounded by a plethora of information and armed with what I now recognise as an overly optimistic attitude of 'can do/will do', I took my first tentative steps toward finding out what all the fuss was about.

A couple of hours and two goggly-eyes later, I closed the books and went out for a beer. With me I took a sinking feeling in the pit of my stomach that didn't feel like it was going anywhere for a while and one burning question: "What on earth were they going on about?"

For the next hour I sat sipping my lager and ruminated on the information I'd been digesting. The first issue I had was that, rather than describing the subjunctive as a tense, many of the books referred to it as a 'mood'. What in God's name did that mean? Of all of the things they said about the Subjunctive, this had to be the least helpful!

Aside from the 'mood' issue, the books described how the subjunctive helped to create uncertainty. Its job was to cast doubt on whether a certain action would happen or not. Now, that I could get my head around! That was easy. All I needed to do was to use the subjunctive when I wasn't really sure that something would happen. '¡Pan comido!' I thought. (A piece of cake.)

Nevertheless, it didn't take long for me to discover that this rule simply didn't hold water. What was worse, there seemed to be more exceptions to the rule than there was compliance to it.

We'll get into the details of all this a little further on, but suffice to say that when I discovered to my horror that any present tense sentence starting with the word "if" *didn't* use the subjunctive, I knew that my 'possible doubt' benchmark was doomed to fail. What could be more doubtful than an 'if'?

What was more, there were just so many rules, regulations, reasons and exceptions to everything that a mere human mind couldn't keep up with them all. (Or at least my human mind.) And even if I could have somehow managed to store all that information away in my head, it would have taken me so long to form a sentence that my poor audience (if I could even keep one) would lose the will to live long before I'd opened my mouth.

Yo contraje 'Subjuntivitis'.

I contracted 'Subjunctivitus'.

However, no matter how much I disliked what I was learning I knew that there was only one way to go forward and that was onwards and upwards. So, with that in mind I stayed as positive as I could and began to work through each and every one of the exercises.

Then, with great determination and, much to the amusement of my Spanish speaking friends, I attempted to wrestle the subjunctive into every conversation I had. I was determined to get to grips with this bothersome tense at whatever cost.

The issue I had at the time, however, was that I was so focused on the subjunctive that it grew into an obsession. Virtually every sentence I created in my head seemed to demand the subjunctive for one reason or another. And so, lamentably, I found myself in the same situation as many of you are in now, as you read this book. I had developed a severe case of terminal 'subjunctivitus'.

And, for more years than I care to count, that's how I remained; confused, frustrated, angry at times and, worse still, over and under using the subjunctive with gay abandon. That was, however, until...

Mi momento bombilla.

My 'light bulb' moment.

...until finally, gloriously, one day I had an epiphany. It was one of those 'light bulb' moments that brought with it a realisation that was to change the entire way I approached the subjunctive.

My moment came whilst I mused over how children learnt language. You see, children don't learn language like adults. Adults like to learn with structure, exercises, heaps of grammar, more exercises; all of which is typically squashed into two hours a week. (Unless, of course, you belong to the 'obsessed' group who tend to work the 'two hours a day' plan.)

Children however, have no concept of what grammar is. They couldn't care less about it. Rather, they limit themselves to learning the patterns of language and repeating those patterns. They make endless mistakes which are patiently (or not so patiently) corrected by their parents and teachers until, finally, they get it right.

What's more, **when children are first learning language they spend little or no time asking the 'why' question**. Rather, they focus themselves on the **'how'** *and the* **'when'***.*

e.g.   When I'm hungry this is how I get food:

"Daddy/Mummy, hungry!"

When I need to use the potty, this is how I tell my parents:

"Daddy/Mummy, potty!"
(But sometimes I keep quiet and just do it in my pants.)

Entonces, ¿cómo nos ayuda eso como adultos?

So, how does that help us as adults?

Having thought this through, I had the feeling that when it came to the subjunctive I had been looking at it from the wrong angle. I'd been trying to understand 'WHY' I had to use it, which as I look back, was tantamount to trying to fit a kangaroo into a letterbox.

What was more, virtually every time I had asked a highly competent native Spanish speaker the 'why' question, the only thing I had received was a look of confusion or a shoulder shrug. Yet, although they struggled to tell me 'why' the subjunctive was used, each and every one of them was an expert at telling me 'when' and 'how' I should use it.

It began to dawn on me that if children didn't ask why they had to say something in a particular way and if the majority of educated Spanish speaking adults weren't able to tell me why I had to use the subjunctive, then perhaps I shouldn't be concerning myself with it either.

Maybe I'd been barking up the wrong tree all that time. Although I knew perfectly well how to create the subjunctive (this will be our first job), knowing 'when' I should use it was my major weakness. What was more, despite the hours I'd spent studying the rules and regulations of the subjunctive, I was still pretty much rubbish at it!

And, so, it was in that moment that I changed the entire way I dealt with the Present and Imperfect (Past) Subjunctive. And it is this method that I am about to share with you; one that will allow you to do the same. Our expectation for you, if you choose to work through this book as we suggest, is that by the time you've reached the end of it you will have lost most of your anxiety around the subjunctive. What's more, the use of the Subjunctive in your spoken Spanish will be correct 90% of the time and you will be recognising it when others use it, too.

Aprender los Detonantes.

Learning the Triggers.

As I have already said, I realised that the big mistake I had been making was trying to understand 'why' the subjunctive needed to be used when really I should have been paying attention to what happened in the language ***just before*** it was used. I needed to know what it was that happened to 'trigger' it off.

And so that's precisely what I began to do. I was amazed at how quickly I noticed a pattern. I saw that just about every time the subjunctive appeared, it was preceded by what I now refer to as a 'trigger'.

This trigger is '***a very specific set of words that 'fire off'*** the subjunctive'.

Now I was getting somewhere! I asked myself if it was possible to learn the triggers and to recognise when they were fired off. The answer, of course, was 'yes', and so began my quest to identify these triggers and classify them into 'families' or groups. What I discovered was that the Spanish subjunctive is 90% logic and 10% art. In this book we will be focusing more on the 90% but, of course, we will take a peek into that fascinating 10%, too.

Lo que no hará este libro.
What this book won't do.

I have spent a lot of time pondering on whether, with each trigger, I should add an extra comment on 'why' we need to use the subjunctive. Finally, I have come to the conclusion that I wouldn't be doing you, the reader, any favours. The reason for this is that for as long as I have been teaching this system, the only time I have come across total confusion in my students has been when they were using their 'why' logic. Invariably, just as I did, they end up forcing subjunctives into the most unlikely of places for the most unreliable of reasons.

And so, that's why we will stick to 'the facts' of 'when' you should use it and not wander off into the mysterious world of 'why'. If, like many people, you are one of those students who must know why you are doing something, then on the Internet alone there are millions of pages that go into eye watering detail on the subject. We will also mention a great book in the bibliography that is filled to the brim with 'whys'.

However, my advice to you right now is to hold your horses a bit; or at least until you've finished working through this book. I'd like to suggest that you focus on this system alone until you have completed all the exercises. Then, once you have everything under control, you can start to look at the whys and wherefores and rules and regulations of the Spanish subjunctive.

A flowchart of your journey through this book.

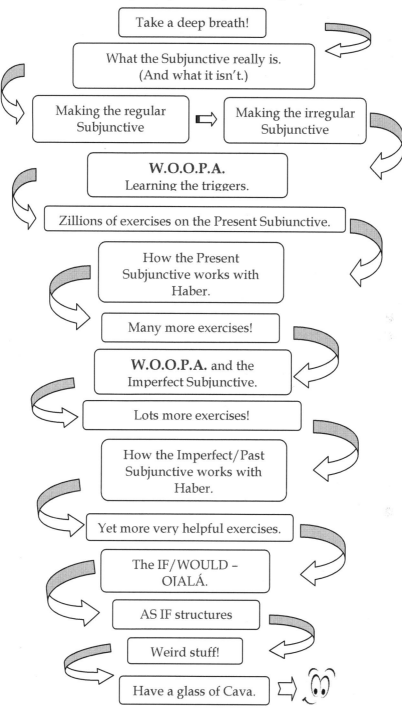

Take a deep breath!

What the Subjunctive really is.
(And what it isn't.)

Making the regular
Subjunctive → Making the irregular
Subjunctive

W.O.O.P.A.
Learning the triggers.

Zillions of exercises on the Present Subjunctive.

How the Present
Subjunctive works with
Haber.

Many more exercises!

W.O.O.P.A. and the
Imperfect Subjunctive.

Lots more exercises!

How the Imperfect/Past
Subjunctive works with
Haber.

Yet more very helpful exercises.

The IF/WOULD –
OJALÁ.

AS IF structures

Weird stuff!

Have a glass of Cava.

¿*Empezamos*?

Shall we start?

 Before we begin to look at the triggers, it's important that you grasp the basic structure of the subjunctive form. In the back of this book you have an index of many of the principle verbs in their subjunctive tenses, however, here we will cover the most important elements that will allow you to understand how to easily create the Present Subjunctive.

Creando el Presente de Subjuntivo.

Making the Present Subjunctive.

A to E...E to A.

The very first thing we are going to learn how to do is to create the Present Subjunctive and, once that's done, we'll give you a working list of the more irregular verbs. (Yes, you guessed it. There are always irregular ones!)

The AR subjunctive structure.

Let's look at the way we make the regular present subjunctive with **AR** verbs.

We'll look at **CAMINAR = TO WALK** as an example.

The very first thing you do to convert an **AR** verb into the present subjunctive is to take the verb down to its **STEM** which in this case is **CAMIN**

Then, all you do is change the **A for an E** in each respective conjugation.

Yo	camin**e**	Nosotros	camin**emos**
Tú	camin**es**	Vosotros	camin**éis**
Él Ella Usted	} camin**e**	Ellos Ellas Ustedes	} camin**en**

Note: The vast majority of AR verbs are as straight forward as this. (Good news, eh?)

Ahora te toca a ti.

Now it's your turn.

Exercise 1.

Here are some regular AR verbs for you to convert to subjunctive. The answers are found in the back of the book.

BAILAR = TO DANCE

Yo _____   Nosotros _____

Tú _____   Vosotros _____

Él ⎫
Ella ⎬ _____   Ellos ⎫
Usted ⎭   Ellas ⎬ _____
     Ustedes ⎭

CONTESTAR = TO ANSWER

Yo _____   Nosotros _____

Tú _____   Vosotros _____

Él ⎫
Ella ⎬ _____   Ellos ⎫
Usted ⎭   Ellas ⎬ _____
     Ustedes ⎭

COMPRAR = TO BUY

Yo _____   Nosotros _____

Tú _____   Vosotros _____

Él ⎫
Ella ⎬ _____   Ellos ⎫
Usted ⎭   Ellas ⎬ _____
     Ustedes ⎭

The ER/IR subjunctive structure.

Now let's look at how we do the same thing with the **ER** and **IR** verbs. These two kinds of verbs have **EXACTLY** the same process.

Let's look at the verbs **COMER** and **VIVIR**.

Just as we did with the **AR** verbs, to convert **ER** and **IR** verbs to the subjunctive we firstly take the verbs down to their stems which are: **COM** and **VIV**

Then, in this case all you do is change the **E for an A** in all the respective conjugations.

Yo	com**a**	Nosotros	com**amos**
Tú	com**as**	Vosotros	com**áis**
Él Ella Usted	com**a**	Ellos Ellas Ustedes	com**an**

Yo	viv**a**	Nosotros	viv**amos**
Tú	viv**as**	Vosotros	viv**áis**
Él Ella Usted	viv**a**	Ellos Ellas Ustedes	viv**an**

Ahora te toca a ti.
Now it's your turn.

Exercise 2.

Convert the following ER and IR verbs to subjunctive.

BEBER = TO DRINK

Yo _____   Nosotros _____

Tú _____   Vosotros _____

Él ⎫
Ella ⎬ _____
Usted ⎭

Ellos ⎫
Ellas ⎬ _____
Ustedes ⎭

LEER = TO READ

Yo _____   Nosotros _____

Tú _____   Vosotros _____

Él ⎫
Ella ⎬ _____
Usted ⎭

Ellos ⎫
Ellas ⎬ _____
Ustedes ⎭

ABRIR = TO OPEN

Yo _____   Nosotros _____

Tú _____   Vosotros _____

Él ⎫
Ella ⎬ _____
Usted ⎭

Ellos ⎫
Ellas ⎬ _____
Ustedes ⎭

ESCRIBIR = TO WRITE

Yo _____ Nosotros _____

Tú _____ Vosotros _____

Él ⎫
Ella ⎬ _____
Usted ⎭

Ellos ⎫
Ellas ⎬ _____
Ustedes ⎭

Y, básicamente, ¡eso es todo!

And that's basically it!

Or, should we say, that's the general idea with some exceptions. (There are always exceptions!) The main difference is found in what we refer to as the **GO-GO** verbs. These are the verbs that change to **GO** in the YO/I form (First person).

Some of these verbs are, for example, **TENER, PONER, HACER**, which, in first person convert to **TENGO, PONGO, HAGO**.

And it's here that we have to give credit and thanks to the very famous, late Michel Thomas, who coined an expression that truly cannot be surpassed and will help you easily remember this simple rule...

The GO-GOs go GA-GA

What that means is that whenever you want to **make the subjunctive form** with a verb that has **GO** in the first person, then you simply change the **GO to GA**.

Here are some examples: (Take note of what is happening to the endings.)

TENER = TO HAVE

Yo	ten**ga**	Nosotros	ten**gamos**
Tú	ten**gas**	Vosotros	ten**gáis**
Él Ella Usted	ten**ga**	Ellos Ellas Ustedes	ten**gan**

PONER = TO PUT

Yo	pon**ga**	Nosotros	pon**gamos**
Tú	pon**gas**	Vosotros	pon**gáis**
Él Ella Usted	pon**ga**	Ellos Ellas Ustedes	pon**gan**

HACER = TO DO

Yo	ha**ga**	Nosotros	ha**gamos**
Tú	ha**gas**	Vosotros	ha**gáis**
Él Ella Usted	ha**ga**	Ellos Ellas Ustedes	ha**gan**

Here are the other principal verbs that do the same as the examples above.

VALER = TO BE WORTH   **DECIR = TO SAY**

VENIR = TO COME   **TRAER = TO BRING**

SALIR = TO GO OUT/LEAVE   **CAER = TO FALL**

Ahora te toca a ti.

Now it's your turn.

Exercise 3.

Have a go at conjugating some of them into the Present Subjunctive:

DECIR = TO SAY

Yo _____   Nosotros _____

Tú _____   Vosotros _____

Él ⎫
Ella ⎬ _____
Usted ⎭

Ellos ⎫
Ellas ⎬ _____
Ustedes ⎭

SALIR = TO LEAVE/GO OUT

Yo _____   Nosotros _____

Tú _____   Vosotros _____

Él ⎫
Ella ⎬ _____
Usted ⎭

Ellos ⎫
Ellas ⎬ _____
Ustedes ⎭

Important note: Many times other verbs that are from the same family or root as those listed above will have the same ending in their subjunctive form. Here are some examples:

IMPONER = TO IMPOSE

Yo	impon**ga**	Nosotros	impon**gamos**
Tú	impon**gas**	Vosotros	impon**gáis**
Él		Ellos	
Ella	impon**ga**	Ellas	impon**gan**
Usted		Ustedes	

CONTENER = TO CONTAIN

Yo	conten**ga**	Nosotros conten**gamos**	
Tú	conten**gas**	Vosotros	conten**gáis**
Él		Ellos	
Ella	conten**ga**	Ellas	conten**gan**
Usted		Ustedes	

REHACER = TO REDO/REMAKE

Yo	reha**ga**	Nosotros	reha**gamos**
Tú	reha**gas**	Vosotros	reha**gáis**
Él		Ellos	
Ella	reha**ga**	Ellas	reha**gan**
Usted		Ustedes	

So, once you know the standard endings of the **GO-GO** verbs, for the most part you can apply them to all of the other similar ones.

Ya basta con todo eso.

That's enough of all that.

For the moment let's leave the construction of the verbs and move on to the fun part! As you go through the exercises you will find a useful index at the back that contains a list of the most important verbs in their subjunctive forms for you to use as a reference.

Una metáfora útil para ayudarte.

A handy metaphor to help you.

Now, before we shoot off into the real 'meat' of the book, it's time to share a metaphor with you which will help you understand how to structure your sentences in the forthcoming exercises.

To start with, here is a classic subjunctive sentence: (It's not important that you understand anything yet. Just look at it.)

Es importante que comas bien.

= It's important that you eat well.

We can break this down into two parts:

Es importante + que

= Subjunctive trigger

comas

= Present Subjunctive.

We'd like you to imagine that every Subjunctive trigger is like a light switch. When the trigger appears, a warning light gets switched on in the sentence. (Or in your head!)

Then, the very next verb that follows on is changed into its subjunctive form, which then switches the warning light off and lets everything go back to normal.

This is pretty much what happens to us as we begin to learn this system. The 'Triggers' appear and switch on a light bulb in our minds. We then act on that trigger by turning the next verb into its correct subjunctive form and that's it, job done and the light goes out again!

Other than the inevitable exceptions that we will cover in detail as we go forward, this is pretty much the entire structure of the Present and Imperfect/Past Subjunctive.

As you work through the many exercises in this book, keep this metaphor in mind. It will serve you well about 90% of the time.

Now, let's get started on the most important part:

Aprender los 'TRIGGERS'

Most of the Subjunctive triggers organise themselves into what we will call in this book, 'families' or groups of expressions that have the same feel or theme. To remember these families, we are going to use the mnemonic:

¡ WOOPA !

This stands for:

Wishes   I hope, If only...etc.

Opinions   It's better that you...It's terrible that...It's fantastic that...etc.

Obligations   It's necessary for him to...There's a need for...There's no need for...

Possibilities   It's possible that...It's probable that...It's doubtful that...

Afterwards   When he arrives...As soon as they come...In case it...

VERY IMPORTANT NOTE:

As you work your way through this book you will be bombarded with many, many different triggers and many ways to say the same thing. Your job is to **choose one or two** triggers from each family. Choose the ones you like or even better, **the ones that you tend to use** in your own speech.

Remember, you don't need to use or remember them all. You just need to be aware of them, so that when you hear someone else using them, you'll recognise them as the subjunctive.

In addition to this, we will make no attempt to fill this book with every possible trigger available. Too many options cause confusion and that is precisely what we want to avoid. In each family of triggers we will offer you a decent range of options to choose from.

<u>Wishes.</u> O. O. P. A.

Let's start with the WISHES family.

This isn't a very large group of expressions, so it's a good place to start.

The Trigger structure is like this:

wish/hope + **QUE** + subjunctive

esperar que ...

to wish/ hope/ expect that ...

esperar a que...

to wait for...

ojalá que ...

if only/I wish ...

Important note:

As you go through the exercises you may notice at times that although you get the subjunctive correct most times, there are times when you don't get the same sentence structure as we do.

This can happen for two reasons. The first, and most important reason, is that there is always more than one way to say something. There are a wealth of similar words and verbs that mean the same thing in Spanish.

Therefore, just because you haven't written what we have doesn't mean that your answer is wrong.

The second reason is that, yes, you could have written a bit of what we like to call, 'SPAMISH'. That's okay, too. As we'll discuss later, throughout the course of the book you will have more than one opportunity to translate the same sentences.

This repetition will help you to make the necessary adjustments to your understanding so that by the end of the book, you will be 'un crack'.

Finally, for those who are learning the Spanish language to use in Latin America and have no use for the 'vosotros' form, in the exercises with 'vosotros' we will also give you the option of using 'ustedes' instead and both options will appear in the answer section.

However, our advice to you is that the world is getting smaller by the minute and so, it's very likely that at some point you will end up talking or listening to a Spanish speaker from Spain and so it might well be worth taking the time to become familiar with the 'vosotros' form just as a backup. We'll leave that decision to you, of course.

Ahora te toca a ti.

Now it's your turn.

Translate the following sentences using these wish triggers.

Exercise 4.

1, I'm waiting for them to arrive.

_____

2, If only she would come today. (venir hoy)

_____

3, They hope that their children pass the exam. (aprobar el examen)

_____

4, She hopes that they make the cake today. (hacer/preparar la tarta)

_____

So, how did you do? Did you get them all correct? If so, well done!

35

Important note: In this part of the book we are dealing only with the present tense and with how the present subjunctive works alongside this tense. Further on, we will start to consider other past tenses. So, if you are thinking, "Yes, but these triggers could refer to the past, too." you'd be right. For the moment, however, put those thoughts on the back burner. We'll get to them soon.

Now, let's talk about an exception to Esperar.

Esperar:

The structure: '**esperar que**' is a trigger for the subjunctive. This is the case whenever we hope for something for someone else, or hope that someone else does something.

However, **when a person hopes for something just _for themselves_ the sentence will _not_ be subjunctive.**

Sidebar comment: I spent a long time trying to figure out how to explain this important exception as easily as I could, so that anyone could understand the rule. I decided that, for you to really grasp it, I needed to show you some examples of what I mean.

However, in the super Spanish grammar book that I have here at home, I discovered an explanation that was clearly written for the benefit of the writer and with little consideration for the non-academic reader:

...a subjunctive subordinate verb is usually only required when the subject of the main verb in the clause and the subject of the subordinate verb are different. (Butt. J., Benjamin. C., A New Reference Grammar of Modern Spanish. 2004.p.248)

So, how do you feel now? Is everything much clearer for you? jeje. Mejor que miremos unos ejemplos. = It's better that we look at some examples.

Examples of Esperar + Verb in Infinitive

Imagine that you want to say:

"I hope that I get good grades."

Here, as you can see, the person (you) is wanting something for themselves.

This is not a trigger for the subjunctive and all you have to say is: "**Espero sacar buenas notas**."

Perhaps you can see from the example that there really is no need to use the subjunctive. In fact, it's much easier to just bolt on your verb to the Esperar conjugation.

The same applies to all the persons in the conjugations. If **any** group of people are hoping for something for themselves then we don't use the subjunctive.

Here are some more examples:

He hopes to see it later. = Él espera verlo más tarde.

(**Not:** Él espera que lo vea más tarde.)

We hope to be teachers. = Esperamos ser profesores.

(**Not**: Esperamos que seamos profesores.)

What do you hope to be? = ¿Qué esperas ser?

(**Not:** ¿Qué esperas que seas?)

Do you get it?

Hoping for something for yourself? Not subjunctive.

Hoping for something for someone else? Subjunctive.

Let's have a little test to see if you've got it.

Note: Some people get confused and think this sentence is hoping for something for oneself:

Espero que me vayan bien los exámenes.

I hope my exams go well for me.

Even though this may seem like you are hoping something for yourself, this isn't the case. You hope the exams go well (they) and so you must use the subjunctive.

Exercise 5

Translate the following sentences:

1, We hope that we hear something soon. (oír algo pronto)

_____

2, They hope that the others arrive on time. (llegar a tiempo)

_____

3, I hope to go to university next year. (ir a la universidad)

_____

4, She hopes that he asks the question. (hacer la pregunta)

_____

5, She hopes to be president of the club. (ser la presidente)

_____

All okay? Could you see the difference between the sentences hoping things for others and those hoping things for the same people?

Great! You'll see when we get to the **Obligations** part of **WOOPA** that the same rule applies to the verb Querer = To want. We'll come to that later, however.

Final note: Esperar has the dual job of meaning 'to wait'. So, even if you make a sentence that talks about waiting rather than hoping, the trigger still works in exactly the same way. The only difference is that you add an 'A'. This works to differentiate between waiting and hoping. Look at this example:

I'm waiting for them to arrive this morning.

Espero **a** que **lleguen** esta mañana.

So, no matter if you are hoping, waiting or expecting, if you use the 'esperar' trigger, you will use the subjunctive.

W. <u>O</u>pinions. O. P. A.

The triggers in this section were the ones that caused me most of my frustration when I was studying the Subjunctive. As I said in the introduction, I used to wrongly imagine that the subjunctive always implied doubt. So when I saw that the following sentence used the Subjunctive I just about flipped out!

How good that you have passed your exam.

Qué bueno que *hayas* aprobado tu examen.

What could be doubtful about that? The exam was passed, of that there was no doubt. Yet, there it was, staring me in the face. The subjunctive used in an extremely non-doubtful way.

Yet, now that we have dispensed with the 'doubt' rule and are just focusing on the 'Triggers' it becomes easy. Give an opinion with this certain structure and, Bob's your uncle, on goes the light and out pops the subjunctive.

In this section we will look at a lot of the triggers that exist around opinions. Just like in English, there are so many different options that we suggest that you only choose to use two or three of them.

There really is no need to overload your mind with too many. After all, we don't use every expression that exists in English either.

The main structure of this opinion trigger is fairly simple.

es/qué + **ADJECTIVE** + **QUE** + subjunctive

Note: Unless we say otherwise, each of these expressions can be used with both 'es' or 'qué' at the beginning, as you can see in some of the examples. It changes the sentences from 'It's' to 'How' but is still a trigger.

e.g.

Es curioso *que* él no hable más del tema.

It's curious that he doesn't talk about the subject more.

Qué curioso *que* él no hable más del tema.

How curious that he doesn't talk about the subject more.

Note: Some of these triggers are often used with 'no' also. For example: 'Es bueno/no es bueno'.

es bueno/ mejor que ...

it's good/ better that ...

es malo/peor que ...

it's bad/ worse that ...

es ridículo que...

it's ridiculous that…

es fantástico que ...

it's fantastic that ...

es increíble que..

it's incredible that…

qué bien que...

how nice that…

es interesante que...	**qué raro que...**
it's interesting that…	how strange that…
es curioso que...	**qué frustrante que...**
it's curious that…	how frustrating that…
qué genial/estupendo que..	**es horrible que...**
how awesome that…	it's horrible that…

And on they go! We could probably fill hundreds of pages with examples if we wanted. To make any kind of Opinion Trigger, all you need to do is follow the same formula and structure as you see above. We said that to create this structure, you only have to add an adjective. However, that rule doesn't apply to just any adjective. You can't, for example, say:

Qué azul que... = How blue that...

So, just use your common sense. Notice that in English, every one of the above examples works. So, use that as your rule of thumb. If you can say that expression in English, then it's very likely that it will work in Spanish too. Likewise, if it won't work in English, it's probably best to avoid it in Spanish too.

Ahora te toca a ti. = Now it's your turn.

Let's practice these Opinion triggers by translating the following sentences into Spanish:

Exercise 6

1, It's incredible that the runners can cover so much distance. (poder cubrir)

_____

2, It's not good that we all think that. (pensar)

_____

3, It's curious that they never look at me. (mirar)

_____

4, How strange that it isn't where I left it. (estar/dejar)

_____

5, How awesome that you're here with me.

_____

Entonces, ¿qué tal este ejercicio? ¿Lo hiciste bien?

If you did, well done! If you struggled a little, don't worry. You'll get plenty opportunities to practise this many times over until you are 'un experto'.

Other Opinion Triggers.

There are some expressions that are still classed as opinions and triggers yet don't have the same structure as the earlier examples. These are the ones in which the word 'es' is produced by the verb, or is replaced by an indirect pronoun (me,te,le,nos,os,les):

(*=triggers that often take a 'no')

opinion verb + **QUE** + subjunctive

(me) cabrea que...
It annoys (me) that...
(It's annoying that...)

*me interesa que...
It interests me that...

*le gusta que...
he/she likes it that...

les encanta que...
they love it that...

me fascina que...
it fascinates me that...

*molesta que...
it bothers that...
(it's bothersome that...)

todo depende de cómo...
it all depends on how...

todo depende de qué..
it all depends on what...

tener miedo de que...
to be scared that...

alegrarse de que...
to be pleased that..

Ahora te toca a ti. = Now it's your turn.

Exercise 6a

Let's practice these Opinion triggers by translating the following sentences into Spanish:

1, It fascinates me that my teacher comes to school on roller boots. (venir/patines)

_____

_____

2, It's annoying that the politicians never answer a question. (contestar)

_____

3, Francisco likes it that his mum prepares spaghetti on Fridays. (preparar/espagueti)

_____

4, It bothers Julia that she can never find her keys. (poder/encontrar)

_____

5, The parents love it that their children come to visit them every week. (venir/visitar)

_____

6, It all depends on how we see it.

7, It all depends on what they do afterwards.

8, I'm scared that the connection will be terrible.

9, I'm happy that my son can draw so well.

¿Ya ves el patrón? No es tan difícil, ¿verdad? Notice that it's not important that the opinion is a positive or negative one. Simply giving any opinion with this structure is your subjunctive trigger.

Just to reiterate the fact that the subjunctive is not always communicating doubt, it was the kind of sentence that we see in number 5 that used to throw me. I would think like this:

The kids come every week. The parents love it. There isn't a shadow of doubt about that! So it must be indicative!

It took me a long time to realise that I had been given what is called in the trade, 'a bum steer'. The subjunctive is not just about casting doubt on things. It's *so much more than that!*

The sooner we dispel that myth about 'doubt' from our minds, the sooner we will begin to understand its use so much more easily.

Watch out for the extended trigger!

Sometimes, we can be caught out by sentences that contain triggers that are under cover. These triggers are often split up so that we don't see the whole structure at first glance.

Take a look at this sentence:

It fascinates me that people, and I'm not talking about people in general but rather the people in my office, don't **take** their responsibilities seriously.

Me fascina que la gente, y no hablo de la gente en general sino de la gente en mi oficina, no **tome** en serio su responsabilidades.

Can you see what happened in that sentence? A trigger was fired off but then the sentence went off on a tangent as the speaker qualified what they meant by 'people'. However, if the trigger is fired off, then the rule is that the next verb that refers to that trigger must be subjunctive. It doesn't matter how much later it appears in the sentence.

Another interesting thing that can happen is that other verbs can appear after the trigger that don't become subjunctive, because they are not part of the actual sentence. They are a qualifying sentence jammed into the original sentence.

Let us show you what we mean:

Qué bueno que Jorge, cuyo padre <u>tuvo</u> ese accidente el otro día y casi se <u>murió</u>, se **mantenga** alegre a pesar de todo.

How good that Jorge, whose father had that accident the other day and nearly died, is **staying** happy despite everything.

This is a classic example of an extended trigger with some other information stuffed into the sentence. The qualifying sentence isn't directly linked to the trigger and so mustn't be changed to subjunctive. Rather, you have to wait until the original sentence picks back up again. Then the verb that applies to that gets changed to subjunctive. Does that make sense?

This kind of structure occurs more in conversation than it does in written texts. That said, we have seen this happen a lot in both written and spoken communication, so watch out for it. However, we don't recommend that you construct your sentences this way as these kinds of structures can be very confusing for the listener. (And to the speaker!)

Giving opinions using 'LO'.

Just like the very first group of opinion triggers that we saw, there is another very similar structure which uses 'LO' and translates closely to 'the thing'. In English we say, "The strange thing is that..." or "The terrible thing is that...".

When this structure is used in Spanish, for the most part, it triggers the subjunctive. Almost always, this happens when the sentence refers to a future event. However, quite often, even when referring to the past, the subjunctive is used too. The rule of thumb is to imagine the sentence seeming more vague or less certain when the subjunctive is used and more definite when the indicative is used. For the sake of clarity here, we will only deal with the subjunctive versions:

LO + opinion adjective + **ES QUE** + subjunctive

Here are some examples:

Lo lógico es que le digan la verdad.

The logical thing is that they tell him/her the truth.

Lo normal es que pases tiempo con tus amigos.

The normal thing is that you spend time with your friends.

Lo raro es que no haga nada para arreglarlo.

The strange thing is that he/she doesn't do anything to fix it.

Here are some examples of these triggers:

lo lógico es que...
the logical thing is that

lo habitual es que...
the usual thing

lo peor es que...
the worst thing

lo malo es que...
the bad thing is that

lo frustrante es que...
the frustrating thing is

lo fascinante es que...
the fascinating thing is

Let's get used to these by doing a few exercises. Translate the following sentences using some of the above triggers:

Ahora te toca a ti.

Exercise 6b

1, The usual thing is that my friends organise a party for me. (organizar)

_____

2, The worst thing is that I don't know what's going on. (saber/pasar)

_____

3, The fascinating thing about all the problems that they have is that they don't do more. (hacer)

_____

_____

4, The logical thing is that they come here first. (venir)

_____

5, The frustrating thing is that nobody thinks about me. (pensar en mí)

_____

Got the idea? If you have then, ¡enhorabuena! If you are still a little hazy, let's do some more exercises to get some practical experience of how all of the Opinion triggers work.

Remember: Once the trigger is fired off, the next verb connected to the trigger will be subjunctive. Then, normally that's it. Job done. (We will get to the sentences that have more than one subjunctive verb later.)

Ahora te toca a ti.

Exercise 6c.

1, It's fabulous that they want to help us. (fabuloso)

_____

2, How sad that she can't come for the wedding. (triste)

_____

3, It's curious that you work so well under pressure. (curioso/bajo presión)

_____

4, How strange, and I don't mean that in a funny way, that I'm eating so much chocolate this week. (raro)

_____

5, It's incredible that there are so many wars in the world. (increíble/guerras)

_____

6, How worrying that they aren't here yet. (preocupante)

_____

7, It's funny that they don't talk to one another any more. (gracioso/ya no se hablan)

_____

8, That they don't come here is very strange. (mixed up, but still a trigger)

_____

9, From my point of view it's terrible that we don't see them these days. (terrible)

_____

10, How frustrating that we can't go there tomorrow. (frustrante)

_____

11, The worst thing is that they don't want to say anything. (decir nada)

_____

12, The logical thing is that you get here for eight tomorrow morning. (llegar para)

_____

How well did you do? Are you getting the idea of the Opinion part of the Triggers?

As we have said and will continue to say, don't allow yourself to become overwhelmed with the quantity of expressions. Really, there are only three basic triggers in the whole of this list:

ES + expression of opinion + QUE + subjunctive

Or

QUÉ + expression of opinion + QUE + subjunctive

Or

LO + expression of opinion + ES QUE + subjunctive

And that's all there is to it!

Now, your job is to choose a handful of your favourite triggers that cover a decent range of positive and negative Opinions and start to practice them in real life.

NOTE: At the moment, what we are doing is focusing you on just one trigger and every sentence that we give you is a classic example of that trigger in action. Once you have all the triggers under your belt, however, we will begin to test you with a mix of them. Then, we will go on to mix trigger and non-trigger sentences together. This will sharpen your ability to decide when you should use the subjunctive and when you should not.

W. O. <u>Obligations</u>. P. A.

This, in our opinion, is a highly used family of Subjunctive Triggers. Maybe it's because we are always trying to oblige others to do things for us!

How we will approach these triggers is to show you the principle patterns within the group.

It's worth noting that the structure and feel of many of the Obligation triggers is like that of the Opinion triggers. The difference is that with the Obligation triggers, you are trying to get someone to do something or to act or think in a certain way.

(That said, Opinion triggers are our way of trying to get others to think our way, too! So, they're not so different.)

As you go forward you will very likely begin to see these patterns repeating themselves over and over again.

Maybe you're not there yet, but once you've worked through this book, you will be far more aware of what we call the 'melody' of the subjunctive. These language structures or triggers as we call them are like notes on a musical scale.

After you've practiced them a lot (And you will, trust us on that!) they will begin to convert into sounds that mesh together just like a well known tune. Every now and then you'll hit a 'bum note' but you'll begin to hear it! And soon you'll be playing the subjunctive like a professional musician.

Now, let's look at the **O**bligation triggers that have the form:

ES + expression of obligation + QUE + subjunctive

e.g.

Es importante **que** me **digas** la verdad.
It's important **that** you **tell** me the truth.

Es preciso **que llamemos** enseguida.
It's necessary **for us** to **call** right away.

*es importante que ...   ***es necesario que ...**
it's important that ...   it's necessary that ...

*es preciso que ...   **es preferible que ...**
it's necessary that ...   it's preferable that ...

*es aconsejable que ...   ***es imprescindible que ...**
it is advisable that ...   it's vital that ...

*es vital que ...   **es innecesario que**
it's vital that ...   it's unnecessary that ...

*Remember that the starred examples can also be used in their negative form.

Ahora te toca a ti.

Exercise 7.

Translate the following sentences from the previous range:

1, It's advisable that she be there for the meeting. (estar para)

_____

2, It's vital that we give him the information. (darle la información)

_____

3, It's necessary that he talk with the doctor soon. (hablar con)

_____

4, It's not important that they know that. (saber eso)

_____

5, It's not necessary that I go with them. (ir/irse)

_____

¿Qué tal? ¿Cómo te fue? Did you get them all correct?

If you did ¡enhorabuena! If you didn't, don't worry. We are just starting out. You will have plenty of opportunity to get more practice as we move forward.

Now we are going to look at some Opinion triggers that take this structure:

Verb of obligation + **QUE** + subjunctive

e.g.

Él **manda que** nos quedemos media hora más.

He **orders us*** to stay half an hour more.

 Yo **sugiero que** lo hagas antes de salir.

I **suggest that** you do it before leaving.

Mi madre me **prohíbe que** cocine sola.

My mum **prohibits me*** to cook alone.

* Have you noticed that sometimes this structure doesn't translate directly into English? The first sentence really has the structure like this:

He **orders that we** stay...

The last one is really:

My mum **prohibits** me **that I** cook alone...

Perhaps we used to speak like that in English a long time ago but not any more. However, Spanish speakers still do. So quite often, when making our sentences in Spanish, we must be aware of their structure. If not, we try to force the English structure into a Spanish sentence and end up with a very Spamish result!

Here are a range of the Obligation triggers with:

verb of obligation + **QUE** + subjunctive

mandar que ...
to order that...

sugerir que ...
to suggest that ...

pedir que...
to ask that ...

prohibir que ...
to prohibit that ...

recomendar que ...
to recommend that ...

rogar que ...
to beg that ...

* querer que ...
to want that...

*conviene que ...
it's advisable that ...

preferir que ...
to prefer that ...

aconsejar que...
to advise that...

decir que..
to say that...(as an order)

To be able to make these trigger sentences, all you need do is to break the verb of Obligation down to the correct person, (the one who is doing the ordering) and add the QUE and then the subjunctive that applies to the person who is being ordered about..

Important note: The trigger: '**conviene que...**' is the only one of the above triggers that doesn't conjugate into different persons. It's used as an 'it's advisable' only. If you want to say: 'I advise that...' you can use: aconsejar que..., recomendar que... or sugerir que...

Even more important note: Just as we saw with the verb Esperar, the verb Querer is only a subjunctive trigger when a person wants something for someone else.

If you want something for yourself, then you don't use the subjunctive. You simply bolt on the verb in its infinitive form.

e.g.

A trigger: I want him to eat. = **Quiero que** él coma.

A non-trigger: I want to eat later. = **Quiero comer** más tarde.

Ahora te toca a ti.

Exercise 8

Translate the following sentences into Spanish:

1, I suggest that you drink it in one go. (beberlo de golpe) (vosotros/ustedes)

_____

2, He recommends that we don't say anything for the moment. (no decir nada de momento)

_____

3, So, you want me to call, do you? (llamar) (usted)

_____

4, I prefer you not to do that here. (hacer) (tú)

_____

5, It's advisable that they only read the first two pages. (leer páginas)

_____

6, I don't want you to come with me tomorrow. (venir conmigo)

_____

7, He wants to stay here. (quedarse)

_____

8, My father prohibits us to go out after nine.

_____

9, I advise you to study this book every day. (estudiar)

_____

10, We recommend that you frequently listen to Spanish. (escuchar frecuentemente) (Do all the 'you' versions)

_____

_____

¿Qué tal este ejercicio? ¿Lo hiciste bien? By now you may be getting the hang of these structures and the way we form the subjunctive.

Don't worry if you don't always get the entire sentence right. This is all a learning process. And what's more, we often learn more from our mistakes then we ever do when we get it right first time.

Now we'd like to show you a few Obligation Triggers that have a slightly different structure but still follow the main theme which is:

statement of obligation + **QUE** + subjunctive

insistir en que ...
to insist that…

más vale que ... ...
it's better that ...

no hace falta que…
There's no need to…

hace que...
it makes that...

dejar que...
to allow that...

e.g.

It's better that we arrive on time.

Más vale que **lleguemos** a tiempo.

There's no need for him to say that.

No hace falta que él **diga** eso.

I insist that she talk in Spanish.

Insisto en que ella **hable** en español.

Ahora te toca a ti.

Translate the following sentences using the above triggers:

Exercise 9

1, It's better that they talk amongst themselves. (hablar entre sí)

_____

2, There's no need for us to finish the work today. (terminar)

_____

3, I insist that they tell me everything. (decir/contar)

_____

4, It's better for you to take it easy. (tomarlo con calma) (tú)

5, There's no need for you to take that attitude. (tomar esa actitud) (ustedes)

6, The mayor insists that the people keep calm. (el alcalde, mantener la calma)

7, Seeing her makes me think of my sister.

8, The teacher often lets the children leave early.

¿Qué tal esta vez? ¿Las has acertado?

Are you noticing the pattern that just keeps repeating itself over and over again?

A **W**ish, **O**pinion or **O**bligation + **QUE** + subjunctive

Have you also noticed that there are many ways of saying the same thing? (And we haven't even given you all of the triggers available!)

Just to say something like: 'It's better that...' we have:

Es mejor que...

Más vale que...

Conviene que...

Es preferible que...

Es aconsejable que...

Note: You **DO NOT** need to use or remember every one of these triggers. After all, they all say more or less the same thing. Why not commit just one of them to memory? Of course, you will hear other people using their favourites, too, but as long as you are familiar with their meaning then that's enough.

Personally, I (Gordon) prefer 'es mejor que' and that's what I use 99% of the time. I still know what others mean when they use the other expressions, I just choose not to use them myself.

Before we move on to our 'repaso' we would like to mention a couple of points on the triggers:

Decir que

and

Insistir en que

These two examples are only triggers for the subjunctive when they are used as an Obligation.

Take a look at these examples:

Insistimos en que asistas a la reunión mañana.

We insist that you attend the meeting tomorrow.

This is subjunctive because it is an Obligation.

Insistimos en que asisten a todas las reuniones.

We insist that they attend every meeting.

This isn't subjunctive because its stating a fact. The fact is that they attend all the meetings without fail. We are insisting that you understand that this is already the case. This might be said if someone was doubting that it were true.

Digo que lo hagas ahora mismo.

I'm telling you to do it right now.

This is subjunctive because the person is obliging the other to do it.

Digo que lo están haciendo ahora mismo.

I'm telling you that they are doing it right now.

This isn't the subjunctive because this is a statement of fact. They are doing it and I'm telling you that.

Can you see the difference? It's only when we are obliging someone that to do something that we would use the subjunctive. If we are simply stating a fact about what is or has happened, then with these two we don't need the subjunctive.

SUCCESS

Súper Repaso- Super Review.

If you are like us, after studying for a while, the things we are learning often get jumbled up in our minds. So, let's have a review of all that we have done up to now. We are going to mix up all the triggers from the Wishes, Opinions and Obligations families.

Ahora te toca.

Exercise 10

1, I want you to stop doing that. (dejar de) (usted)

_____

2, If only they would decide. (decidir)

_____

3, It's better that you don't listen to that. (escuchar) (tú)

_____

4, I'm begging you to see my point of view. (ver mi punto de vista) (ustedes)

_____

5, I hope I pass the exam. (aprobar)

_____

6, It's not important that you start at eight in the morning. (empezar) (vosotros/ustedes)

_____

7, It's curious that she wants to wait a few months. (esperar)

_____

8, They hope that the police arrive quickly. (llegar)

_____

9, It's vital that you read the entire letter. (leer) (ustedes)

_____

10, I prefer that they don't get up until later. (levantarse)

_____

¿Cómo te fue este último ejercicio?

If you were considering whether the trigger belonged to the Obligation or Opinion families, did you find yourself unsure?

That's because with some of the triggers, like:

Es preferible que...

...the way you use them and their context can change their meaning.

For example, if your boss said that to you, it would be much more like an obligation than if a friend were to say the same thing.

Does it matter? Not at all!

Whatever the family, it's a trigger and so the subjunctive has to be used anyway. The idea of the families is simply to create some kind of easy structure for you to use as a reference.

However, they are not written in stone and can be flexible, just as we have to be when we learn a language.

W. O. O. <u>Possibilities.</u> A.

Before we launch into this next family of triggers, it's important that we touch on the word IF which is SI in Spanish. I recall this causing me no end of problems when I studied the subjunctive.

The reason why it's a bit tricky is because SI has two big jobs that in many ways are contradictory.

One of its jobs is to **take away** the need for the Present Subjunctive. This is the one that we will be dealing with now.

The other job it has is to form part of a special trigger that involves the Past or Imperfect Subjunctive. For the moment, let's focus on the present tense and on how the use of SI affects the sentence.

I used to assume that if a sentence started with the word 'IF' then it had to be subjunctive. And yet, exactly the opposite is true here.

Look at these examples:

If they come by nine it'll be fine.

Si **vienen** para las nueve estará bien.

If he says that to her again she'll be angry.

Si se lo **dice** a ella otra vez se enfadará.

If you want to go to see the show I'll pay for the ticket.

Si **quieres** ir a ver el espectáculo, yo pagaré la entrada.

There are two points that you should bear in mind about SI as a non-subjunctive trigger. Notice in the sentences that we have made that they are all in present tense. This is an important point to remember when we get to the special IF/WOULD constructions later.

Also, it is important to understand that, in present tense sentences, the SI only affects the verb that follows it. If triggers appear later in the same sentence, they are NOT affected by the word SI and are still triggers. We'll show you some examples of this later.

Now let's take a look at first group of triggers that are used to indicate possibilities and in this family we include doubts. Again, there tends to be a structure to them:

ES + verb of possibility + **QUE** + subjunctive

By now you probably aren't very surprised that this family of triggers has this kind of structure! ¿Verdad?

Here are the main ones:

es imposible que ...
it's impossible that ...

es improbable que ...
it's unlikely that ...

es posible que ...
it's possible that ...

no es seguro que ...
it's not certain that ...

es dudoso que ...
it is doubtful that ...

es incierto que ...
it's uncertain that ...

es difícil
it's unlikely

es probable que ...
it's probable/ likely that ...

no es verdad que ...
it's not true that ...

e.g.

Es posible **que** no **venga.**

It's possible that he is not coming.

No **es** seguro **que** lo **vea** así.

It's not certain that she sees it like that.

Ahora te toca.

Exercise 11

Let's practice the above Possibility/Doubt triggers now. There is more than one possible answer in some of the sentences!

1, It's impossible that they know what is happening. (saber)

_____

2, It's doubtful that I can do that for next week. (hacer)

_____

3, It's probable that we will be there on Monday. (estar)*

_____

4, It's likely that you will have problems. (tener) (usted)*

_____

5, It's possible that they'll tell me in the morning.

_____

6, It's not true that he wants to see it.

_____

7, It's uncertain that the dentist can see you right away.

_____

8, It's unlikely that we'll win the lottery.

_____

* We have starred some of the above sentences because we think it's worth while taking some time out to talk about them. These are the kind of subjunctive sentences that seem to cause the most confusion with our students.

Why?

Probably because of the way that we use the future tense in English. Look at this sentence:
It's probable that **we will** be there on Monday.

At the beginning, when I (Gordon) was faced with a sentence like this, I would conjugate the verb into the future, like this:

Es probable que (nosotros) **estaremos** allí el lunes.

My logic worked like this: 'I WILL', well, you can get much more certain than that, can you? Therefore, I should use the 'will' tense. (Wrong again, of course!)

No matter how sure you are that you will be or do something, if that '**will**' word is **preceded by a subjunctive trigger**, then you will use the subjunctive.

The same applies if you were to translate that sentence from Spanish to English. You would swap the subjunctive verb for a future verb.

e.g.

Es posible que **estemos** aquí para las nueve.

becomes:

It's possible that **we will** be here for nine.

So, watch out for that. Don't be fooled into using the future tense with a trigger just because that's what we do in English.

Extra Note: Now, let's get serious for a moment. Look at all of the Possibility Triggers. Do you think it's really necessary for you to use all of them to express a possibility or doubt? They are all virtually the same. At most you should be choosing two to use in the future. Any more and it's just a waste of brain space!

Now, let's look at the next type of trigger in the Possibilities family. This has a slightly different structure, but by now, not one you are unfamiliar with:

verb of doubt + **QUE** + subjunctive

e.g.

Dudo que yo vaya.
I doubt I'm going.

No me imagino que sea verdad.
I don't imagine that it's true.

And, here are some of the main triggers in this part of the Possibilities family:

no pensar que ...
to not think that ...

no creer que ...
not to believe that ...

dudar que ...
to doubt that ...

no imaginarse que ...
to not imagine that ...

no suponer que ...
to not suppose that ...

negar que ...
to deny that ...

puede ser que ...
it may be that ...

no decir que...
not saying that...

el hecho de que...
the fact that...
(We will cover this later.)

no significar que...
doesn't mean that...

74

The Non-Triggers

In the previous list there are some triggers that can also become non-triggers if you make them positive. You must be aware of these so that you don't unnecessarily use the subjunctive when the indicative is required.

Take a look at these examples:

Pensar and No Pensar

Pienso que no **es** perjudicial. = **Non-Trigger**
I think it's not harmful.

No pienso que sea perjudicial. = **Trigger**
I don't think it's harmful.

Creer and No Creer

Creo que él no **tiene** la lista. = **Non-Trigger**
I think/believe that he doesn't have the list.

No creo que él **tenga** la lista. = **Trigger**
I don't think that he has the list.

Imaginarse and No Imaginarse

No se puede **imaginar** que ella **haga** eso. = **Trigger**
One/you can't imagine that she would do that.

Se puede **imaginar** que ella **hace** eso. = **Non-Trigger**
One/you can imagine that she would do that.

Suponer and No Suponer

El profesor **no supone que** a los alumnos les **interese** la tarea. = **Trigger**
The teacher doesn't suppose that the students are interested in the homework.

El profesor **supone que** a los alumnos les **interesa** la tarea. **Non-Trigger**
The teacher supposes that the students are interested in the homework.

Decir and No Decir

No decimos que el plan **sea** perfecto. **Trigger**
We aren't saying that the plan is perfect.

Decimos que el plan **es** perfecto. **Non-Trigger**
We are saying that the plan is perfect.

The Special Rules for Dudar and Negar.

When it comes to the use of these two verbs we enter into the strange and mysterious world of the 10% of art that we mentioned in the introduction to this book.

We have seen that the structures:

'Dudo que...' and **'Niego que...'**

demand the use of the subjunctive.

However, even when these structures are changed from doubt and denial to no doubt or denial, most Spanish speakers will still use the subjunctive.

Take a look at these examples:

Dudo que sea un buen cocinero. **Trigger**
I doubt that he is a good cook.

No dudo que sea un buen cocinero. **Trigger**
I don't doubt that he is a good cook.

El ayuntamiento **niega que** el proyecto **tenga** problemas.
Trigger
The council denies that the project has problems.

El ayuntamiento **no niega que** el proyecto **tenga**
problemas. **Trigger**
The council don't deny that the project has problems.

So, what's going on here? Well, beforehand, when I thought that the subjunctive only dealt with doubt, I found the whole idea of using the subjunctive with sentences like: I don't doubt... quite amazing / frustrating / confusing / annoying etc.

However, once I understood about trusting the triggers, it became easier to manage.

Just out of interest, however, if you think about how we use these kinds of sentence constructions in English, very often we inject an element of doubt into them. How many times have we said:

"I don't doubt that you care but I'm just not feeling it."

Although the words we use talk about not doubting, our tone of voice and our use of the word BUT (Behold the Underlying Truth) show our real opinion.

**"I don't deny that you've made an effort but it just
wasn't good enough."**

And, so it's this kind of sarcastic feel of saying one thing and meaning another that we find in these triggers.

El hecho de que... The fact that...

It may seem strange that we have included an expression that on the face of it is quite the opposite of doubt. Yet, just like the 'no doubt' trigger, 'el hecho de que...' is more frequently used with subjunctive.

Why?

Basically, if we consider the following sentence we can perhaps see how it has a very similar feel to the 'no doubt' structure:

The fact that you are intelligent doesn't give you the right to talk to me that way.

El **hecho de que seas** inteligente no te da derecho a hablarme así.

Can you notice the 'feel' that this sentence has? Perhaps you are starting to get the sense of what the subjunctive communicates. It's sometimes difficult to put into words (hence it's called a 'mood' and not a 'tense'.)

It's almost as though the sentence could be said this way:

The fact that **you might be** intelligent doesn't give you the right to talk to me like that.

Does that make sense? Just as we said at the beginning of this book, it's best if we put out of our mind that the subjunctive conveys doubt because as a benchmark, it's not solid enough to rely on.

However, what's interesting about the above sentence is that the doubt that this sentence conveys isn't about whether the person is or isn't intelligent. It simply puts into question the right that the person has to talk a certain way despite their intelligence.

It's for this reason that it's best not to over analyse and ask 'why'. Rather, we should for the moment focus just on learning the triggers. (Most Spanish speakers wouldn't know why they use the subjunctive in this sentence, just that they do!)

So, let's have a review of this family of Possibilities / Doubts triggers, but pay special attention to this exercise because it contains non-triggers, too.

Ahora te toca a ti.

Exercise 12

Translate the following sentences into Spanish:

1, My neighbour believes that I'm not going to Spain to live.

_____

2, I don't doubt that the crisis will end soon. (acabarse)

_____

3, I don't imagine that I'll get married before you. (casarse/tú)

_____

4, The fans don't deny that their team has problems. (los fanáticos)

_____

5, I suppose that the grandparents will be able to go to the show.

_____

6, My boss doesn't think that we deserve a pay rise. (merecerse/aumento de sueldo)

_____

7, Do you doubt that I'm capable of doing it? (tú)

_____

8, They just don't imagine that it can be possible.

_____

9, I'm not saying that Elizabeth can't do it.

_____

10, We believe they can't do it and their coach doesn't believe they can do it either.

_____

_____

11. Your teacher doesn't deny that you work hard in class. (tú)

_____

12, I'm saying that the staff do that today.

_____

13, The fact that she lives here isn't an excuse.

14, This is a bad situation but it doesn't mean that there isn't a solution.

¿Cómo vas con estos ejercicios? ¿Ya has cogido el ritmo?

Can you see the pattern that just keeps repeating itself over and over again?

Have you noticed, also, the critical role that QUE has in the Triggers?

It's not used every time, but pretty much 95% of the examples need it to create the trigger. And this is where the problems start...

Subjuntivitus.

It's worth taking a moment to talk about the issue that we all have at times, which is our seeing the need for the subjunctive everywhere, in every sentence.

However, just because QUE appears in the majority of triggers doesn't mean that it is a trigger in and of itself.

For QUE to trigger off the need for the subjunctive there have to be other elements present.

If you look at all of the formulas that you have used up to now, you will see a very fixed pattern. Take a look now:

wish/hope	+ **QUE**+subjunctive
ES/QUÉ + opinion adjective	+ **QUE**+subjunctive
opinion verb	+ **QUE**+subjunctive
LO + opinion adjective	+ **ES QUE**+subjunctive
ES + obligation adjective	+ **QUE**+subjunctive
obligation verb	+ **QUE**+subjunctive
ES + possibility verb	+ **QUE**+subjunctive
possiblity verb	+ **QUE**+subjunctive

So, as you can see from the above table, from what we have covered so far, **QUE** only creates a trigger when it is accompanied by verbs or adjectives of **W**ish/Hope, **O**pinion, **O**bligation, **P**ossibility/Doubt. Using QUE in a sentence that doesn't have these elements *will not normally* create a trigger.

Now, let's take a look at the last couple of possibility / doubt triggers, without which Spanish wouldn't be the same.

quizá/quizás...   **tal vez..**
perhaps/maybe…   perhaps/maybe

These work like this:

Quizá(s) me **tome** un café más tarde. = Maybe I'll have a coffee later.

Tal vez **venga** mi padre a arreglarlo. = Maybe my father will come to fix it.

The thing about Quizá/s...

Let's firstly clear up any confusion over QUIZÁ and QUIZÁS. There is no difference between them and you can use them interchangeably. Another interesting thing about quizá as a trigger is that it doesn't always have to be a trigger for the subjunctive.

If you want to, you can use the normal present tense (indicative) with it. However, when you do that the meaning changes a little.

When you use *the subjunctive* with QUIZÁ/S, you are showing that *it's quite doubtful* that something will happen.

If you use *the indicative*, present tense with QUIZÁ/S you are showing there *it's more likely* to happen.

Look at these examples.

Quizá **venga** mañana. = Maybe he/she is coming tomorrow. (But it's less likely.)

Quizás **viene** mañana. = Maybe she/he is coming tomorrow. (It's more likely.)

Ahora te toca.

Exercise 13

Let's practice these two Possibility words now. Translate the following sentences to Spanish:

1, Maybe my sister will be at the party on Friday. (Less likely.)

_____

2, Maybe you know better than me. (Less likely.)

_____

3, Perhaps I'll leave you in the shopping centre. (Less likely.)

_____

4, Perhaps we'll find out next week. (Enterarse) (Less likely.)

_____

5, Maybe the machine is broken. (estar roto) (More likely.)

_____

¿Cómo te ha ido todo? ¿Crees que entiendes los Triggers de Posibilidad? ¡Qué bien!

Now comes the big one! Let's practice all of the Triggers we have covered up to now.

We did say that by the time you've finished this book you will have the confidence to use the subjunctive and the only way we can fulfil that promise is through practice.

84

Así que....¡a por ello!

Te toca de nuevo.

Exercise 14

Translate the following sentences into Spanish:

1, The man denies that he forgets a lot. (olvidar)

_____

2, The town hall insist that the lights go out at eleven. (apagarse)

_____

3, It's probable that nobody will arrive until after ten. (llegar)

_____

4, It's advisable that everyone wears a lifejacket. (llevar/un chaleco salvavidas)

_____

5, The teacher orders that all the children be quiet. (callarse)

_____

6, I beg you not to talk with him again. (hablar con/tú)

_____

7, The logical thing is that you buy this car right now. (comprar/tú)

_____

8, It's fantastic that both the men are talking to one another now. (hablarse)

_____

9, It fascinates him that his children know so much. (saber)

_____

10, It's annoying that we pay so many taxes. (pagar impuestos)

_____

11, It interests me that you think that. (pensar/tú)

_____

12, If only she would pay attention to me. (prestar atención)

_____

13, We love it that our friends are so interesting.

_____

14, There's no need for you to say anything. (decir/usted)

_____

15, The soldiers don't believe that they are winning the war. (ganar/guerra)

16, The young girl hopes to go to Spain to see a friend. (ir/se)

17, Maybe I'm wrong. (estar equivocado) (It's fairly certain.)

18, It's impossible that those shapes are people. (formas/ser)

19, We prefer that you don't see him any more. (verlo/ya no/tú)

20, How horrible that not even you can tell me the truth. (decir/ni siquiera/la verdad/usted)

21, The boss doesn't doubt that his staff need a break.

22, The child believes that his friends don't want to spend time with him.

23, I don't deny that I am involved.

24, They imagine that they won't go to Spain again.

25, I don't doubt that he's a good teacher.

¡Fiúuuu! ¿Estás sudando? ¿Qué tal te fue? ¿Bien? Esperamos que sí.

The subtle *Possibility* Triggers that catch us out.

Now that you have all of that under your black-belt, so to speak, we'd like to cover a Subjunctive Trigger that falls into the small percentage of the very subtle triggers that often catch us out.

Let us show you some examples of it in action. Perhaps you've seen it before:

1, Do you have any work that I can do?

¿Tienes algún trabajo que yo **pueda** hacer?

2, They don't have anything that can fix it.

No tienen nada que **pueda** arreglarlo.

3, Is there anyone that speaks English here?

¿Hay alguien aquí que **hable** inglés?

4, In this group there isn't anyone who knows what happened.

En este grupo no hay nadie que **sepa** qué pasó.

5, I'm looking for a person that cleans swimming pools.

Busco una persona que **limpie** piscinas.

6, Do you know anyone who knows how to fix cars?

¿Conoces a alguien que **sepa** arreglar coches?

So, precisely, what do we have here? Are you a little puzzled? Don't worry! We will now look at each example and see what the triggers are. Then we'll practice them to help you get a feel for it.

Let's take a look at example number 1 and 2.

The key triggers are these:

The question.

> ¿Tienes algún trabajo que **pueda** hacer yo?

¿**Tener** + something/someone + **QUE** + subjunctive?

And

The statement.

> No tienen nada que **pueda** arreglarlo.

No +Tener + something/someone + **QUE** + subjunctive

Why are these triggers in the Possibilities group? We have placed them here because we suggest that you could add into these sentences (at a squeeze) the word 'might':

Do you have any work that I **'might'** be able to do?

They don't have anything that **'might'** be able to fix it.

Let's take a look at example number 3 and 4.

The key triggers are these:

The question.

¿Hay alguien aquí que **hable** inglés?

¿**Hay** + something/someone + **QUE** + subjunctive?

And

The statement.

En este grupo no hay nadie que **sepa** qué pasó.

No + Hay + something/someone + **QUE** + subjunctive

Once again, these could well be Possibilities if you think a little creatively and add the words, 'may' and 'might':

Is there anyone that **'might'** speak English here?

In this group there isn't anyone who **'may'** know what happened.

Important note: Many of you may be thinking that this possibility idea wouldn't hold water if, for example, we 'really knew' that nobody knows anything.

Imagine that we've asked all of the people involved and everyone has said that they know nothing. Why would we then use the subjunctive?

The answer comes back to what we said right at the beginning. It's best not to get into the question of doubt or no doubt. It makes you get things wrong.

The fact is, to a Spanish speaker's ear, this is the correct melody. This is what is used in this kind of sentence. It's the structure, or the Trigger that dictates the need for the subjunctive and not the level of doubt.

If you really did want to communicate the fact that nobody knows anything, then you would choose another kind of structure to say that. For example:

En este grupo **nadie sabe nada** sobre lo que pasó.

In this group, nobody knows anything about what happened.

Can you see the difference between example 4 and the one above? No triggers are fired off in the above sentence and so we can use the indicative.

Now let's look at the next example, number 5, which was:

I'm looking for a person that cleans swimming pools.

Busco una persona que **limpie** piscinas.

So, what is the trigger here?

Buscar + something/someone + **QUE** + subjunctive

Likewise, here, we could also tentatively add a 'might' into the sentence, making it fit into the Possibility family:

I'm looking for a person who '**might**' clean pools.

On a similar line let's take a look at the last example, number 6.

Do you know anyone who knows how to fix cars?

¿Conoces a alguien que **sepa** arreglar coches?

What is the trigger here?

Conocer (a) + someone + **QUE** + subjunctive

Once again, it would be possible to put into this sentence the word 'might':

Do you know anyone who '**might**' know how to fix cars?

Mixing with SI/IF.

Watch out that you don't get fooled by sentences of this kind that have the word IF/SI in them which, as we know, neutralises the need for the subjunctive if used in the present tense form.

Take a look at this sentence:

Do you know if there's anyone around here who can fix boilers?

¿Sabes si hay alguien por aquí que **pueda** arreglar calderas?

Did you notice that although SI figures in the sentence, we still have the subjunctive? The reason for that is because the 'SI' only affects the verb that comes directly afterward it, which in this case is 'hay' of 'haber'. However, we see that the 'hay' forms a trigger for the subjunctive as we have seen it do in the earlier examples:

Hay + someone/thing + **QUE** + subjunctive

So, it's worthwhile making a mental note that the word SI/IF doesn't take away the need for the subjunctive in the entire sentence, only from the verb that follows it.

Exercise 14a

Ahora te toca a ti.

Let's practice these particular structures now:

1, The boss doesn't have any job that I can do right now.

_____

2, Is there a phone around here where I can make a call?

_____

3, Do they know anyone who works with animals?

_____

4, Do you have anything that I can make to eat? (usted)

_____

5, I'm looking for a secretary who has a lot of flexibility.

_____

6, There's nothing you can drink here. (tú)

_____

7, Do we have anything that we can give them?

_____

8, The ice-cream seller doesn't have anything that you want. (ustedes)

_____

9, Is there somewhere I can get a shower?

_____

10, Do you know anyone who makes made to measure clothing.

_____

¿Qué tal?

As we said, this is one of the subtle triggers that often catch us out. However, practice makes perfect.

Now, let's move on to the last Trigger in our list.

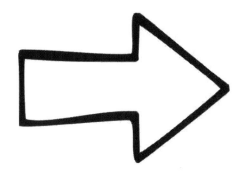

W. O. O. P. <u>Afterwards</u>.

So, what do we mean by 'afterwards'?

Well, what we are talking about are events that are up-and-coming. These are the things that will happen in the future. However, before we look at them let's make one thing clear...

Talking about future events is NOT an automatic trigger for the subjunctive.

As always, there has to be a fixed structure. Up to now we have only briefly touched on the non-triggers. Our focus has been on what it is that actually triggers off the subjunctive. However, as we look at this family, we have no choice than to look at the one that on first glance creates the most confusion:

cuando ...
when ...

Now, we are sure that as you look at this trigger you must be thinking... 'OMG...I'm constantly using 'when' in Spanish and I haven't once used the subjunctive with it. Does that mean I've been wrong all this time?

And the answer is, no! This word, **cuando**, is only a trigger when you use it in a very special way.

cuando + a up and coming event = subjunctive

Here are some example sentences:

Cuando (me) **vaya** a Perú, voy a quedarme en un hotel de cinco estrellas.
When I go to Peru, I'm going to stay in a five-star hotel.

Cuando recibas la tarjeta, avísame.
When you **get** the card, tell me.

Cuando me lo **digan**, lo sabré definitivamente.
When they **tell** me, I'll know for certain.

Can you see the pattern? It's simply that we use **CUANDO** followed by an **event in the future**.

When it isn't a Trigger.

When you use the word 'when' followed by repetitive, every day, routine events, you don't need to use the subjunctive. Here are some examples:

Cuando **hablo** con mi hermano siempre me cabreo.
When I talk with my brother I always get angry.

No me gusta cuando **tengo** que esperar en una cola. *

I don't like it when I have to wait in line/in a queue.

* Did you think for a moment that 'No me gusta cuando..' was a trigger? It's not! The trigger you may have thought about is: 'No me gusta que...'.

For a sentence to be a trigger it must have the exact structure that we have shown you. Don't worry too much about this. We will be practicing how to identify a trigger/non-trigger later on.

Cuando **estoy** en España, como en el restaurante cerca de mi apartamento.

When I'm in Spain I eat in a restaurant close to my apartment.

Have you identified the pattern of when you use 'cuando' without the subjunctive?

It's simply this:

Cuando + habitual event = **indicative** (normal present tense)

¡Te toca!

Exercise 15

Okay, let's practice fine tuning your ability to identify when 'when' is a trigger and when it isn't.

Translate the following sentences paying special attention to whether the sentences are really triggering off the subjunctive (when they refer to a future event).

1, When we eat in my family's house, we often have chicken.

_____

2, When we eat in my family's house tomorrow, we will have chicken.

_____

3, When we go on holiday we'll take lots of sun-cream.

_____

4, When we go on holiday we take lots of sun cream.

_____

5, When you drive on Saturday, take care.

_____

6, When you drive you normally take care.

_____

7, When they talk to me they smile.

8, When they talk to me they'll smile.

9, When we are in Spain, we'll visit the beach.

10, When we are in Spain, we visit the beach.

¿Qué tal el ejecicio? ¿Pudiste identificar las diferencias? If you managed to do so, then well done! If you didn't, well done for having a go. Of all of the triggers in the Afterwards family, this one is probably the one that causes most confusion.

We'll be doing some more on these in the review.

The 'cuando' exception.

Like so many things we learn in Spanish, we have to be aware that there are nearly always exceptions to the rule.

It is possible to use 'when' and a future event without having to use the subjunctive.

Look at these sentences:

¿Cuándo **vas** a hablar con él?
When are you going to talk with him?

Entonces, ¿cuándo te **vas** a Colombia?
So, when are you going off to Colombia?

Neither of these sentences needs the subjunctive. But why?

Well, there is a subtle distinction between these sentences and the '*cuando*'+ *subjunctive* sentences that we have practiced. (This used to catch me out a lot! (Gordon))

This is how you can identify this exception:

1, It's a question specifically about when someone is going to do something. (It is asking for **a time, day or date**.)

2, It uses one of the **three kinds** of Spanish **future**.

Here are some examples:

¿Cuándo van a ir al centro?
When are they going to go to the town centre?

¿Cuándo van al centro?
When are they going to the town centre?

¿Cuándo irán al centro?
When will they go to the town centre?

Answer: Mañana por la mañana.

Here are some more examples:

¿Cuándo vas a ir a comer?
When are you going to go to eat?

¿Cuándo vas a comer?
When are going to eat?

¿Cuándo comerás?
When will you eat?

Answer: A las tres.

Now look at this question:

Entonces, **cuando estés** en Panamá, ¿**cuándo vas** hablar con ese hombre?

So, when you are in Panama, when are you going to talk with that man?

Can you see that the sentence starts with a 'cuando' trigger. How do we know that?

Because the structure is 'cuando' + future event.

The question is not asking 'when?' the person is going, but rather, it is referring to the future event. This **IS** a trigger.

The second part is a specific 'when' question that requires a time, day or date answer. This **IS NOT** a trigger.

Another way to look at it is that when you form the sentence in the subjunctive, it can't stand alone like the indicative 'when' question.

e.g.

When you go to Spain...?
(This sentence needs more. It's incomplete.)

When are you going to Spain?
(This is a complete sentence that doesn't need anything else.

Let's practice identifying the difference between the two kinds of 'when' sentences.

¡Ahora te toca!
Exercise 16

1, When will they arrive?

_____

2, When they arrive will there be cake?

_____

3, When are we going to watch the movie/film?

_____

4, We will order a pizza for when we watch the film/movie.

_____

5, When will you read the book? When you are in Spain? (tú)

_____

6, I don't know when she'll arrive.

_____

7, When she arrives we can talk about the plans.

_____

8, When you get the information will you inform me please? (usted)

_____

9, I'll call you when I'm at the office. (tú)

_____

10, When will you be in the office? (usted)

_____

¿Cómo vas con estos ejemplos? ¿Puedes ver la diferencia?

Qué bien☺ We know that it can be a little confusing but you needn't worry. All these exercises are programming the patterns into your mind. Before you know it you'll be forming sentences with these kind of structures and surprising your own self.

More *AFTERWARDS* triggers with *QUE*.

Here are some more 'Afterwards' triggers, below, that have what is now becoming a very familiar QUE in their structure.

Take time to look at what these triggers are doing. Notice how, in one way or another, they are referring to future events that haven't happened yet.

reference to a future event + **QUE** + subjunctive

a menos que ...
unless ...

antes (de) que ...
before ...

con tal (de) que ...
as long as/ so that ...

sin que ...
without ...

mientras (que) ...
while/ as long as ...

hasta que ...
until ...

después (de) que ...
after...

para que ...
in order to.../so that...

en caso de que ...
in case ...

a no ser que...
unless...

una vez que...
once...

lo que...
whatever... (only for future)

aunque...
even if/although...

(The words in brackets can be omitted.)

Ahora te toca.

Exercise 17

Have a go at translating these sentences using the above Triggers:

1, I'm taking an umbrella in case it rains. (llover)

2, We are going to eat at three unless you are hungry now. (tú)

3, The guys are going to the bar after they eat.

4, Don't leave without paying. (Usted.)

5, The girls are waiting until we get there.

6, I'll do it as long as it makes you happy.(tú)

7, Whilst you are here can you fix that light? (Usted.)

8, So that it works, we have to fill the machine with water. (funcionar)

9, Give me that before it breaks. (romperse) (tú)

10, Once we tell them, we can do it.

11, You can have whatever you want at the party.

_____

12, Even if she comes here to ask me directly, I won't do it.

_____

¿Cómo te fue el ejercicio? ¿Ya empiezas a capturar la idea?

In many respects, after having spent so long teaching the subjunctive, we can understand what the great wise ones meant when they said that it was a 'mood'.

There's a certain feel to the subjunctive that appears and reappears in each family. It's difficult to put into words. It's like a feeling of uncertainty / doubt / possibility that permeates each sentence.

This is why you may have found that one family of triggers seems to blur into another. We feel the same.

It's for this reason that students (and many teachers) wrongly work on the premise that if there's a doubt then we should use the subjunctive. The fact is, though, that there's a much more rigid structure to it than that.

As you have seen, for the subjunctive to be triggered there must be a very specific set of words beforehand. Without those words or that structure, there is no trigger.

Recently a student said to me (Gordon):

"Lo siento pero no vaya mañana."

I asked her why she had chosen to add the subjunctive to the sentence. She replied that it was because she wasn't sure whether she was going or not.
She thought that the 'no vaya' part of the sentence meant: "I may not go."

Her error was thinking that just changing a verb to the subjunctive turned it into a 'maybe'. As you have seen from all the previous exercises, that simply isn't the case. Also, perhaps you've noticed that most verbs in the subjunctive translate into English as if they were normal indicative verbs.

So, what would be the correct way to say what our student wanted to say?
Lo siento, **es posible que** no vaya mañana.

To create the doubt, you **have to add** the doubt structure.

Remember:
The subjunctive isn't what necessarily creates the doubt; it's there to let you know that doubt is present.

So now let's take a look at a couple of other Afterwards triggers that have slightly different structures:

en cuanto ...   **tan pronto como ...**
as soon as .../once...   as soon as ...

It's worthwhile making a mental note of one of these triggers as they tend to be used a lot!

¡Ahora te toca a ti!

Exercise 18

Translate these sentences using the above triggers:

1, As soon as the builder gives us a date we can make a plan.

_____

2, Once my father falls asleep I'll call you. (dormirse) (tú)

_____

3, As soon as I know more, I'll tell you. (ustedes)

_____

4, Once the president signs, it's all over. (acabarse todo)

_____

5, As soon as we sit down you can begin to serve the food. (ustedes)

_____

When is an Afterwards Trigger not a Trigger?

Because this group deals with future events/afterwards, then the Triggers that you have seen all fire off when you use them to refer to future events.

However, with 'en cuanto' and 'tan pronto como' there are times when you aren't talking about future events but rather, everyday, repetitive actions.

Look at the difference between these two sentences:

As soon as I arrive I'll call.
En cuanto/tan pronto como **llegue**, llamaré. **Trigger**

As soon as I arrive I call.
Tan pronto como/en cuanto **llego**, llamo. **Non-Trigger**

What is the difference here? The first sentence is clearly referring to a time in the future. You can tell that by the use of the future "I'll call".

The second sentence isn't talking about the future. It's talking about repeated actions. You can tell that by the use of the present. "I call".

A great way of knowing if you are referring to the future is by trying to add the word 'ALWAYS'. If it works in the sentence, it will NOT be subjunctive.

Let's try that with the above sentences:

As soon as I arrive I'll always call. (This sounds wrong)

As soon as I arrive I always call. (This sounds okay)

Ahora te toca a ti.

Have a go at identifying which sentences contain the triggers.

Exercise 18a

1, As soon as the police arrive we'll tell them everything.

_____

2, As soon as they arrive we go straight to the garden.

_____

3, As soon as we get the ball we run as fast as possible.

_____

4, As soon as we get the ball we'll attack.

_____

5, As soon as the priest arrives, we'll sit down.

_____

¿Qué tal el ejercicio esta vez? ¿Sabes? Vas muy bien y puedes estar muy orgulloso/a de tu trabajo hasta la fecha. Esperamos que sigas progresando y aprendiendo.

The First Big Step Completed!

¡Qué guay! You've reached the end of what we might call the standard Present Subjunctive. You've seen a great range of triggers in each family, although by no means have you seen them all. (We don't want this book to be as thick as the Pillars of the Earth by Ken Follet.)

Before we move on, let's review the Afterwards family of triggers with a mix of them all.

Okay, breathe in deeply and let's check out your learning once more. Oh, and by the way, it's perfectly normal for you to have to look back through the book for the triggers.

¡Ahora te toca!

Exercise 19

1, We can't go until they give us the keys.

_____

2, As long as the doctor signs me off today, I'll be at work tomorrow. (Dar el alta.)

_____

3, I always drink water when I eat.

_____

4, I'll call you as soon as my friends go. (tú)

_____

5, I can't help you unless you tell me what's wrong. (tú)

_____

6, Here, take this money with you in case you have to buy something. (ustedes)

_____

7, At least have a coffee while you're here with me. (tú)

_____

8, As soon as I retire I'm off to Mexico. (jubilarse)

_____

9, What do you do that for? So that the food has a nice flavour. (tú)

_____

10, Without knowing it, you are saying exactly what I think. (usted)

_____

11, We must get bread before we go back home.

_____

12, When I eat today, I'm going to have a big steak.

_____

13, I'll have whatever there is.

14, Whatever! (ser) (They say, whatever it may be.)

15, As soon as I get into my car I put on my seat belt.

¡Fiúuuu!

¿Qué tal te fueron estas frases? ¿Todo bien?

Well, we have to give you the ¡enhorabuena! You've completed the first and most important part of learning to use the Subjunctive with ease.

You see, now that you've seen the triggers in action, you are simply going to see them repeated over and over again in other tenses. The great thing is that what doesn't change is the basic structure.

Remember: **Once a trigger, always a trigger.**

So, where do we go to now? Would you believe that it's time for a full review and more exercises. However, in this book we are going to use a special technique for reinforcing the learning called 'The Power of Three.'

The Power of Three.

This is a great system which is used to really drive home any kind of message. It's used everywhere, especially in advertising (because they really want you to remember their products). It works a bit like this:

1, Tell them what you're going to tell them.

2, Tell them.

3, Tell them what you've told them.

This 'Power of Three' system is very effective with language learning. Let me explain why.

I recall (Gordon) studying what I consider to be a great book called Spanish Verb Tenses by Dorothy Denvey Richmond. Although it's well structured it's a BIG book with many exercises on every tense in the Spanish language.

The first time I studied it, it took me about 6 weeks to work through the book. Although I went through it with real focus, by the time I'd finished the last chapter I couldn't remember anything that I'd covered in the earlier part of the book.

I was very disappointed with myself and wondered what was wrong with me. Somewhat frustrated, I had no choice than to start once more at the beginning and do the exercises again. Fortunately, I had used a pencil and so I could erase the previous answers I'd written. (That took me about an hour!)

That said, although I had rubbed out the answers, I could still make out what I'd written previously. However, rather than being a problem, this actually gave me great feedback. Because I could see my previous answers, I was able to see that I wasn't making anywhere near the same amount of errors the second time around.

I had obviously learnt from my mistakes, but it was the act of doing the exercises for the second time that helped me appreciate the learning that had taken place.

I was so impressed with how much the review was helping me that, once I was done, I repeated the book for the third time. (I must stress that I had a break between the second and third session. I am not a masochist!)

As I went through the book for the last time I quite literally flew through it! Every sentence was easy! I had become familiar with what I had learnt, I was getting just about everything correct and as a consequence my confidence soared.

This is 'The Power of Three'.

We want you to feel that way too! So, what we will do in this book to help you achieve the same great result is to repeat the exercises, all be them a little mixed up. We won't be giving you different sentences, rather, they'll be the same ones as before. Why? Because this will give you the opportunity to *learn from your previous errors and reinforce your successes.*

By the time you reach the end of this learning journey, you will have completed the same exercises three times. When you finish, what you know you will know well. You will have each family of triggers clear, solid and making all the right noises in your head.

What's more, you'll have had time to choose your own favourite triggers out of each family and you'll feel confident to use them.

In addition to that, you'll begin to notice when other Spanish speakers use the Subjunctive and you'll find yourself making Subjunctive sentences unconsciously and with ease.

Súper Mega Repaso.

So, let's get on with reinforcing your learning with our súper repaso of the entire range of **W.O.O.P.A.** triggers.

Here are all of the exercises you've completed up to now. All we've done is change their order a bit.

Please, take the time to do them again. You'll be amazed at how accurate your answers will be compared to your first time around.

Note: If you really don't want to go through all of the exercises again, (but we recommend that you do so) then why not choose the ones that challenge you the most.

Así que, prepárate. Buena suerte y ¡a por ello!

Exercise 7.

1, It's advisable that she be there for the meeting. (estar para)

_____

2, It's vital that we give him the information. (darle la información)

_____

3, It's necessary that he talk with the doctor soon. (hablar con)

_____

4, It's not important that they know that. (saber eso)

_____

5, It's not necessary that I go with them. (ir/irse)

_____

Exercise 10

1, I want you to stop doing that. (dejar de) (usted)

_____

2, If only they would decide. (decidir)

_____

3, It's better that you don't listen to that. (escuchar) (tú)

_____

4, I'm begging you to see my point of view. (ver mi punto de vista) (ustedes)

_____

5, I hope I pass the exam. (aprobar)

_____

6, It's not important that you start at eight in the morning. (empezar) (vosotros/ustedes)

_____

7, It's curious that she wants to wait a few months. (esperar)

_____

8, They hope that the police arrive quickly. (llegar)

_____

9, It's vital that you read the entire letter. (leer) (ustedes)

_____

10, I prefer that they don't get up until later. (levantarse)

_____

Exercise 4.

1, I'm waiting for them to arrive.

_____

2, If only she would come today. (venir hoy)

_____

3, They hope that their children pass the exam. (aprobar el examen)

_____

4, She hopes that they make the cake today.
(hacer/preparar la tarta)

Exercise 14a

1, The boss doesn't have any job that I can do right now.

2, Is there a phone around here where I can make a call?

3, Do they know anyone who works with animals?

4, Do you have anything that I can make to eat? (usted)

5, I'm looking for a secretary who has a lot of flexibility.

6, There's nothing you can drink here. (tú)

7, Do we have anything that we can give them?

8, The ice-cream seller doesn't have anything that you want. (ustedes)

_____

9, Is there somewhere I can get a shower?

_____

10, Do you know anyone who makes made to measure clothing.

_____

Exercise 8

1, I suggest that you drink it in one go. (beberlo de golpe) (vosotros/ustedes)

_____

2, He recommends that we don't say anything for the moment. (no decir nada de momento)

_____

3, So, you want me to call, do you? (llamar) (usted)

_____

4, I prefer you not to do that here. (hacer) (tú)

_____

5, It's advisable that they only read the first two pages. (leer páginas)

_____

6, I don't want you to come with me tomorrow. (venir conmigo)

_____

7, He wants to stay here. (quedarse)

_____

8, My father prohibits us to go out after nine.

_____

9, I advise you to study this book every day. (estudiar)

_____

10, We recommend that you frequently listen to Spanish. (escuchar frecuentemente) (Do all the you versions)

_____

_____

_____

_____

Exercise 14

1, The man denies that he forgets a lot. (olvidarse)

2, The town hall insist that the lights go out at eleven. (apagarse)

3, It's probable that nobody will arrive until after ten. (llegar)

4, It's advisable that everyone wears a lifejacket. (llevar/un chaleco salvavidas)

5, The teacher orders that all the children be quiet. (callarse)

6, I beg you not to talk with him again. (hablar con/tú)

7, The logical thing is that you buy this car right now. (comprar/tú)

8, It's fantastic that both the men are talking to one another now. (hablarse)

9, It fascinates him that his children know so much. (saber)

10, It's annoying that we pay so many taxes. (pagar impuestos)

11, It interests me that you think that. (pensar/tú)

12, If only she would pay attention to me. (prestar atención)

13, We love it that our friends are so interesting.

14, There's no need for you to say anything. (decir/usted)

15, The soldiers don't believe that they are winning the war. (ganar/guerra)

16, The young girl hopes to go to Spain to see a friend. (ir/se)

_____

17, Maybe I'm wrong. (estar equivocado) (It's fairly certain.)

_____

18, It's impossible that those shapes are people. (formas/ser)

_____

19, We prefer that you don't see him any more. (verlo/ya no/tú)

_____

20, How horrible that not even you tell me the truth. (decir/ni siquiera/la verdad/usted)

_____

Exercise 19

1, We can't go until they give us the keys.

_____

2, As long as the doctor signs me off today, I'll be at work tomorrow. (Dar el alta.)

_____

3, I always drink water when I eat.

_____

4, I'll call you as soon as my friends go. (tú)

_____

5, I can't help you unless you tell me what's wrong.

_____

6, Here, take this money with you in case you have to buy something. (ustedes)

_____

7, At least have a coffee while you're here with me. (tú)

_____

8, As soon as I retire I'm off to Mexico. (jubilarse)

_____

9, What do you do that for? So that the food has a nice flavour. (tú)

_____

10, Without knowing it, you are saying exactly what I think. (usted)

_____

11, We must get bread before we go back home.

_____

12, When I eat today, I'm going to have a big steak.

_____

13, I'll have whatever there is.

_____

14, Whatever! (ser) (They say, whatever it may be.)

_____

Exercise 13

1, Maybe my sister will be at the party on Friday. (Less likely.)

_____

2, Maybe you know better than me. (Less likely.)

_____

3, Perhaps I'll leave you in the shopping centre. (Less likely.)

_____

4, Perhaps we'll find out next week. (Enterarse) (Less likely.)

_____

5, Maybe the machine is broken. (estar roto) (More likely.)

_____

Exercise 6a

1, It fascinates me that my teacher comes to school on roller boots. (venir/patines)

_____

2, It's annoying that the politicians never answer a question. (contestar)

_____

3, Francisco likes it that his mum prepares spaghetti on Fridays. (preparar/espagueti)

_____

4, It bothers Julia that she can never find her keys. (poder/encontrar)

_____

5, The parents love it that their children come to visit them every week. (venir/visitar)

_____

6, It all depends on how we see it.

_____

7, It all depends on what they do afterwards.

_____

8, I'm scared that the connection will be terrible.

_____

9, I'm happy that my son can draw so well.

Exercise 9

1, It's better that they talk amongst themselves. (hablar entre sí)

2, There's no need for us to finish the work today. (terminar)

3, I insist that they tell me everything. (decir/contar)

4, It's better for you to take it easy. (tomarlo con calma) (tú)

5, There's no need for you to take that attitude. (tomar esa actitud) (ustedes)

6, The mayor insists that the people keep calm. (el alcalde, mantener la calma)

7, Seeing her makes me think of my sister.

_____

8, The teacher often lets the children leave early.

_____

Exercise 18

1, As soon as the builder gives us a date we can make a plan.

_____

2, Once my father falls asleep I'll call you. (dormirse) (tú)

_____

3, As soon as I know more, I'll tell you. (ustedes)

_____

4, Once the president signs, it's all over. (acabarse todo)

_____

5, As soon as we sit down you can begin to serve the food. (ustedes)

_____

Exercise 5

1, We hope that we hear something soon. (oír algo pronto)

_____

2, They hope that the others arrive on time. (llegar a tiempo)

_____

3, I hope to go to university next year. (ir a la universidad)

_____

4, She hopes that he asks the question. (hacer la pregunta)

_____

5, She hopes to be president of the club. (ser la presidente)

_____

Exercise 18a

1, As soon as the police arrive we'll tell them everything.

_____

2, As soon as they arrive we go straight to the garden.

_____

3, As soon as we get the ball we run as fast as possible.

_____

4, As soon as we get the ball we'll attack.

_____

5, As soon as the priest arrives, we'll sit down.

Exercise 11

1, It's impossible that they know what is happening. (saber)

2, It's doubtful that I can do that for next week. (hacer)

3, It's probable that we will be there on Monday. (estar)*

4, It's likely that you will have problems. (tener) (usted)*

5, It's possible that they'll tell me in the morning. (decírmelo)

6, It's not true that he wants to see it.

7, It's uncertain that the dentist can see you right away.

8, It's unlikely that we'll win the lottery.

_____

Exercise 6c.

1, It's fabulous that they want to help us. (fabuloso)

_____

2, How sad that she can't come for the wedding. (triste)

_____

3, It's curious that you work so well under pressure. (curioso/bajo presión)

_____

4, How strange that I'm eating so much chocolate this week. (raro)

_____

5, It's incredible that there are so many wars in the world. (increíble/guerras)

_____

6, How worrying that they aren't here yet. (preocupante)

_____

7, It's funny that they don't talk to one another any more. (gracioso/ya no se hablan)

8, That they don't come here is very strange. (mixed up, but still a trigger)

9, From my point of view it's terrible that we don't see them these days. (terrible)

10, How frustrating that we can't go there tomorrow. (frustrante)

11, The worst thing is that they don't want to say anything. (decir nada)

12, The logical things is that you get here for eight tomorrow morning. (llegar para)

Exercise 15

1, When we eat in my family's house, we often have chicken.

2, When we eat in my family's house tomorrow, we will have chicken.

_____

3, When we go on holiday we'll take lots of sun-cream.

_____

4, When we go on holiday we take lots of sun cream.

_____

5, When you drive on Saturday, take care.

_____

6, When you drive you normally take care.

_____

7, When they talk to me they smile.

_____

8, When they talk to me they'll smile.

_____

9, When we are in Spain, we'll visit the beach.

_____

10, When we are in Spain, we visit the beach.

_____

Exercise 6

1, It's incredible that the runners can cover so much distance. (poder cubrir)

_____

2, It's not good that we all think that. (pensar)

_____

3, It's curious that they never look at me. (mirar)

_____

4, How strange that it isn't where I left it. (estar/dejar)

_____

5, How awesome that you're here with me.

_____

Exercise 16

1, When will they arrive?

_____

2, When they arrive will there be cake?

_____

3, When are we going to watch the movie/film?

_____

4, We will order a pizza for when we watch the film/movie.

_____

5, When will you read the book? When you are in Spain? (tú)

_____

6, I don't know when she'll arrive.

_____

7, When she arrives we can talk about the plans.

_____

8, When you get the information will you inform me please? (usted)

_____

9, I'll call you when I'm at the office.

_____

10, When will you be in the office?

_____

Exercise 6b

1, The usual thing is that my friends organise a party for me. (organizar)

_____

2, The worst thing is that I don't know what's going on. (saber/pasar)

_____

3, The fascinating thing about all the problems that they have is that they don't do more. (hacer)

_____

4, The logical thing is that they come here first. (venir)

_____

5, The frustrating thing is that nobody thinks about me. (pensar en mí)

_____

Exercise 17

Have a go at translating these sentences using the above Triggers:

1, I'm taking an umbrella in case it rains. (llover)

_____

2, We are going to eat at three unless you are hungry now. (tú)

_____

3, The guys are going to the bar after they eat.

_____

4, Don't leave without paying. (Usted.)

_____

5, The girls are waiting until we get there.

_____

6, I'll do it as long as it makes you happy.(tú)

_____

7, Whilst you are here can you fix that light? (Usted.)

_____

8, So that it works, we have to fill the machine with water. (funcionar)

_____

9, Give me that before it breaks. (romperse) (tú)

_____

10, Once we tell them, we can do it.

_____

11, You can have whatever you want at the party.

_____

12, Even if she comes here to ask me directly, I won't do it.

_____

Exercise 12

Translate the following sentences into Spanish:

1, My neighbour believes that I'm not going to Spain to live.

_____

2, People doubt that the crisis will end soon. (acabarse)

_____

3, I don't imagine that I'll get married before you. (casarse/tú)

_____

4, The fans deny that their team has problems. (los fanáticos)

_____

5, I don't suppose that the grandparents will be able to go to the show.

_____

6, My boss doesn't think that we deserve a pay rise. (merecerse/aumento de sueldo)

_____

7, Do you doubt that I'm capable of doing it? (tú)

_____

8, They just don't imagine that it can be possible.

_____

9, I'm not saying that Elizabeth can't do it.

_____

10, We believe they can't do it and their coach doesn't believe they can do it either.

_____

_____

11. Your teacher doesn't deny that you work hard in class. (tú)

_____

12, I'm saying that the staff do that today.

_____

13, The fact that she lives here isn't an excuse.

_____

14, This is a bad situation but it doesn't mean that there isn't a solution.

_____

How was that marathon review? Did you notice that this time around you were much more accurate?

Did you recognise a change in your feelings toward the subjunctive? Perhaps it feels more familiar or it looks more manageable now. Are certain triggers ringing bells for you now?
That's great. There really is no substitute for repetition when learning a language and if you stick with this, you'll find that all your hard work will pay off with a great, confident Spanish.

The Extended and the Double Trigger

Now is probably a good time to talk about the sentences that contain more than one subjunctive verb in them. Perhaps you've noticed them and felt a little confused. That's normal!

I recall being totally confused about how much of the sentence the subjunctive trigger actually affected. Did it just affect the verb that follows directly after? Did it affect all the verbs in the sentence? How could I know?

Fortunately, there are answers to all of those questions.

There are two main times when more than one verb in the Subjunctive will appear in a sentence.

Let's look at the first case which we will call *the Extended Trigger:*

Her parents want her to study and work hard.

Sus padres quieren que ella **estudie** y que **trabaje** duramente.

What has happened here?

Well, what we have seen is that an **O**bligation trigger has been fired off (quieren que...). However, the girl's parents don't just want her to do one thing, but rather they want her to do a couple of things.

Here's another example:

I hope that the neighbours don't make too much noise and that the party ends before twelve.

Espero que los vecinos no **hagan** demasiado ruido y que la fiesta **termine** antes de las doce.

Again, we see a **W**ishes trigger firing off the need to use the subjunctive. However, this time the person is hoping for two things.

Of course, there is no limit to how many things you can wish for in a sentence. However, we don't recommend that you make the list overly long (imagine wishing for ten things to happen in one sentence). Making your subjunctive sentences too long tends to confuse your listener (and you).

So, you can use any one trigger to fire off a series of subjunctive verbs. All you need to do to add more **WOOPA**'s is to follow this structure.

TRIGGER + QUE + SUBJ + Y QUE...etc.

Exercise 20

Try this out with the following sentences:

1, The dog likes its owners to spend time with him, walk him every day and give him good food.

_____

_____

2, María thinks that it is strange that her boyfriend doesn't call and doesn't visit her as much as before.

_____

_____

3, As soon as I finish painting and making the dinner, I'll go to pick you up. (tú)

_____

_____

4, It's possible that the boys are in their class now and can't answer their phones.

_____

_____

Do you get the idea? Great!

Now, let's look at the other most common case in which we see the subjunctive repeating itself in the same sentence.

We'll call this the *Double Trigger.*

Look at this sentence:

The boss thinks* **it's terrible that** you never arrive on time and **he wants** you to explain yourself now.

El jefe piensa/cree que **es terrible que** nunca **llegues** a tiempo y **él quiere que** te **expliques** ahora.

* Pay special attention to the fact that this sentence starts with a non-trigger, which we will touch on later, and yet it still has the subjunctive in it. Why? Because no matter what comes beforehand, if a trigger is fired off (in this case, 'it's terrible that') then the subjunctive WILL follow.

Can you see that in the above sentence, two triggers are fired off and two subjunctives are used in response to those triggers?

Of course, you aren't tied to one trigger per sentence. As long as you maintain understanding, you can add as many triggers as you like. At the beginning, however, we suggest that you keep one trigger to a sentence. This is purely for your own comfort and is far easier to manage.

Try out these sentences with *double triggers*.

Exercise 21

1, Unless they tell you, you can always ask them to give you an extra day. (tú)

_____

_____

2, After we arrive do you want us to do anything in particular? (usted)

_____

_____

3, How frustrating that they don't want us to be there tomorrow. *

_____

4, It's ridiculous that we pay so many taxes when all we need is that they provide the basic services.

_____

_____

5, The fascinating thing is that we can choose whatever we like.

_____

_____

* Have you noticed a curious thing about the starred sentence? Did you see that the second trigger in the sentence was actually a verb in the subjunctive too?

'no quieran que...'

So, what can happen in these double trigger sentences is that the first trigger affects the second, making it subjunctive. Whatever, the case, whether a trigger is in the indicative or in the subjunctive, it still counts as a trigger.

Here are a couple more examples of this curious structure:

I'm asking you to suggest to José that he reads the entire exam.

Te **pido que** le **sugieras a José que lea** el examen entero.

It's vital that we don't think that the children are worth less than we are.

Es imprescindible que no pensemos que los niños **valgan** menos que nosotros.

Now that you've seen how this works, let's do a few of these kind of sentences:

Exercise 22.

1, It's advisable that the head teacher prohibits that the students use mobiles in the classroom.

_____

_____

2, How terrible that the partners are saying that the investors must withdraw their money.

_____

_____

3, As long as it is important that we know that information, we should learn it well.

_____

_____

 Okay, that's probably enough on this kind of structure for the moment. What you will find happening as you develop your Subjunctive skills is that you will gradually move from simple sentences to more complex ones.

At the beginning, however, it's enough that you use ONE correctly in any given sentence. I still recall my first 'live' sentence with the subjunctive in it. I was talking to a Spanish couple and I said this:

Me falta la práctica aquí en Inglaterra porque **no hay** mucha gente **que** hable español.

I remember it to this day for two reasons:

1, I was over the moon that I had actually managed to use the subjunctive correctly and especially whilst talking with two Spaniards.

2, I had no blessed idea why I needed to use it in that sentence!

Looking at the sentence, now, can you see why we use the Subjunctive? Which of the W.O.O.P.A. family would that construction fall into?

It's pretty much one of the subtle Possibility sentences that we covered on page 88. It has the classic structure of:

no hay + (something) + que + subj

The other important point to remember, as we have mentioned, is that this book does not contain all of the triggers that ever existed. It would be too long and too complex if it did.

What we are doing is giving you the key trigger types. As you get them ingrained into your brain you will begin to see lots of variations of the same thing.

The best way for you to deal with them as you come across them is to simply ask yourself which family they would fit into and try to use them a couple or three times.

And, of course it goes without saying, avoid asking yourself why!

Now, having covered all of that it's time for us to leave the present tense and move on to how the Present Subjunctive works with Haber.

Buena suerte, chicos. ☺

The Present Subjunctive
with HABER and
the Present Perfect
(The 'I have eaten' tense.)

Now it's time to take ourselves to the next level of competence. Here we are going to learn how the **W.O.O.P.A.** family works with the Present Perfect tense and the verb HABER = to have (done).

Just like any other verb, HABER has its own subjunctive conjugation. It's a fairly irregular verb in present so it's not surprising that it's irregular in the present subjunctive too.

This is how it conjugates:

HABER = TO HAVE DONE

Yo	**haya**	Nosotros	**hayamos**
Tú	**hayas**	Vosotros	**hayáis**
Él Ella Usted	**haya**	Ellos Ellas Ustedes	**hayan**

Just as a reminder, this 'have eaten' tense with the Present Subjunctive is made up of two parts. The HABER conjugation, as you have just seen, and what is called the 'Past Participle'.

Apart from the irregular verbs, the Past Participle (eaten, taken, talked, walked, flown, etc.) is made up like this:

AR verbs

Drop the AR and add ADO

e.g. **Hablar** = to speak/talk **Hablado** = spoken/talked

ER/IR verbs

Drop the ER/IR and add IDO

e.g. **Comer** = to eat   **Comido** = eaten

Vivir = to live   **Vivido** = lived

What we will do now is to look at how some of the **W.O.O.P.A.** triggers work with this tense.

It may be surprising to hear (or not) that most triggers can be used with the Present Perfect tense. Therefore, rather than wading through every one of the triggers again, we will cover some from each group so you can get the idea. Then you can do what you're getting best at and get down to practicing them.

Examples of **W**ishes with the PP.

I hope that she has finished the cake.

Espero que ella **haya terminado** la tarta.

She hopes that Maria has waited a little longer.

Espera que María **haya esperado** un poco más.

Can you see that, in terms of structure, there is little difference between the sentences in present tense and those using the present perfect? The triggers still stand and all that happens is that it is the verb Haber that changes to the Subjunctive.

Examples of **O**pinions with the PP.

It's curious that they haven't called yet.

Es curioso que todavía no hayan llamado.

It's fantastic that you have passed your exam.

Es fantástico que hayas aprobado tu examen.

It annoys me that he hasn't even told me.

Me cabrea que ni siquiera me lo haya contado.

The teacher likes that his students have all arrived on time.

Al profesor le gusta que todos sus estudiantes hayan llegado a tiempo.

The weird thing is that the council hasn't sent us any letter.

Lo raro es que el ayuntamiento no nos haya enviado ninguna carta.

Examples of **O**bligations with the PP.

It's important that the workmen have finished by six.

Es importante que los obreros hayan terminado para las seis.

It's vital that you have taken your medicine.

Es vital que te hayas tomado tu medicina.

It's necessary that the staff have all received the safety training.

Es preciso que todo el personal haya recibido el entrenamiento de seguridad.

It's advisable that everyone has eaten before we head off to the theatre.

Conviene que todos hayamos comido antes de irnos al teatro.

Examples of Possibilities with the PP.

It's very possible that you haven't heard properly what he said to you.

Es muy posible que no hayas oído bien lo que él te dijo.

I don't think that we have done our best work here today.

No creo que hayamos hecho nuestro mejor trabajo aquí hoy.

The farmers doubt that they have been treated well by the government.

Los granjeros dudan que el gobierno los haya tratado bien.

I don't suppose the papers have arrived.

No supongo que hayan llegado los papeles.

Examples of Afterwards with the PP.

After the electrician has finished with the lights, we'll start painting.

Después de que el electricista haya terminado con las luces empezaremos a pintar.

Without having seen it, you won't believe it.

Sin que lo hayas visto, no lo creerás.

As long as you have passed your entrance exam, the job is yours.

Con tal de que hayas aprobado el examen de ingreso, el trabajo es tuyo.

It's as simple as that.

So, perhaps you have noticed how, although we are using a different tense, we still have the same triggers creating the same need for the subjunctive.

Haber is a verb just like any other and thus it behaves just like any other.

Let's practice a little bit now with a complete mix of Triggers. Don't worry if you have to flip back through the book to find the right trigger. However, after having repeated them twice already, you will probably find that many of them will come to mind easily.

Exercise 23

1, How awesome that the team have won for the third time.

_____

2, Unless Elena has written it herself, I can't accept it.

_____

3, It interests Guillermo that all of his friends have grown beards. (dejarse crecer)

_____

4, My parents-in-law love that they have been able to see their grandson every day.

_____

5, The politician denies that he has been involved in the dirty business of accepting bribes.

_____

6, Leticia doubts that her husband has remembered her birthday.

7, It's better that you have spoken with Diego before he leaves for Paris. (tú)

8, Cristina prefers that the dogs have had their walk before nine o'clock.

9, Mari Carmen says that it's important that all of the people have arrived by twelve.

10, The logical thing is that you have seen the papers before the lawyer arrives. (ustedes)

¿Qué tal te fueron estos ejercicios? Did you manage them well? As we progress, you'll find the sentences getting a little more challenging. Don't worry. With the *power of three* system you'll have them totally sorted by the end of the book.

And, really, as for dealing with the Present Perfect tense (The 'I have eaten' tense) that's about all there is to it! Whatever happens, the W.O.O.P.A. triggers apply as much to this tense as they do to the Present Indicative tense (The 'I eat' tense.) although some triggers lend themselves more easily to certain tenses.

We are wondering how you are feeling about the subjunctive at this point. Perhaps these exercises have helped to answer a lot of questions that you've had. It's also possible that they have created even more questions in your mind. It's also likely that, because we haven't finished explaining everything yet, you are more confused about certain things than you were before you started the book. (By the way, we could never explain everything in one book!)

And we are here to tell you that all of these things are fine. The nice thing about confusion is that it is normally followed by 'clarity'. Cynthia and I have always welcomed the state of confusion into our learning journey. (As if we had a choice in the matter!)

Despite what you might think, one of the most stuck states to be in during your Spanish learning journey is the state of 'total confidence'. Now, that may sound a little strange. Surely, having confidence makes you a better speaker, doesn't it?

Well, that depends. Confidence based on a deep knowledge of your subject is great. However, confidence coming from a basis of very little knowledge isn't so good. They do say that a little knowledge is a dangerous thing! Don't get us wrong, we aren't saying that it's bad to be confident; we are simply saying that true confidence comes from a full understanding of your subject.

You see, we have noticed over the years that many people who are completely new to learning languages display far more confidence when using their Spanish than some people who have been learning for years. Why is that?

It's because generally, beginners 'don't know that they don't know'.

The Levels of Learning

Perhaps this might be a good moment to take time out to talk about *how* we learn. Once you understand how the mind moves through the learning process then you can begin to see where you are on your own personal learning journey. Understanding this will make everything clearer for you and may well help you to be more patient with yourself in the future.

In the model that we use as a reference, there are 4 levels to learning:

1, Unconscious Incompetence.

2, Conscious Incompetence.

3, Conscious Competence.

4, Unconscious Competence.

1, Unconscious Incompetence. (Ignorance is bliss.)

This is the very first level of learning and it means that we are unaware of what we know. ***We don't know that we don't know***. We've never tried to learn Spanish, for example, and so we have no reference of whether we can learn a language or not. We could be good at it. We could be rubbish. We simply don't know because we haven't tried. This is the level at which some people display their misplaced confidence. e.g. "Yeah, I'm really good at Spanish. I can say: Dos cervezas en uno plástico vaso, por favor."

2, Conscious Incompetence. (The painful truth.)

This is the learning level in which we normally have our 'Shock/Horror' moment. We finally pluck up the courage to start to learn Spanish, we attend our first class, open our first book and, BAM! Suddenly, it all looks like a foreign language to us. What's worse is that we discover we didn't even know our own language too well either. This is the moment in which we realise that *We know that we don't know.* It is this realisation that often wipes out 75% of the students in our beginner's Spanish classes.

Typically, the class starts out with 20 people, all blissfully ignorant and ready to 'give this Spanish a try'. By the end of the first or second tri-semester, however, that jolly group has shrunken down to what usually amounts to 5 stalwart members. These are the people who stare level two in the face and continue on despite everything. You, the person reading this book now, were one of those select few. Congratulations to you on getting through to the next level!

3, Conscious Competence. (Makes my brain hurt.)

After having applied yourself and studied assiduously, you finally get to level three. This is the point in which you conceptually understand what you have learnt and you can create a sentence to be proud of, if you are given enough time. And that's the problem; everything is just so painfully slow. The entire process of getting coherent sentences to come out of your mouth is nothing short of impossible.

You know that you know, but it just doesn't flow. If you dare to take your mind off the ball for even a second, the weirdest of things come flying out of your mouth. What's more, the poor people obliged to listen to you whilst you cobble sentences together look like they are about to fall asleep, and stifle yawns behind glazed eyes. In addition to that, when you are at this level, after about half an hour of talking in Spanish, you have to go and have a lie down.

This is because you are talking consciously. That's not how we talk in our mother tongue. Rather, we talk unconsciously without thinking. It's easy and painless. Talking consciously, however, is like learning to drive. The instructor informs us that we need to check the mirror, depress the clutch (for the stick shift people), put the car into gear, check the mirror again, accelerate, get the bite on the clutch just right without jolting the car, check the mirror again, put the indicator on, find a gap in the traffic, take off the hand brake, ease out into the tiniest gap possible, turn off the indicator....well, you get the idea. We look at them as though they are mad! "You want me to do what?"

At the time we can't conceive that a human mind could manage to do all of those things at once. Yet, one year later we find ourselves doing all of that whilst, at the same time, searching for our favourite station on the radio, checking our hair in the mirror, reaching for something under our seat and holding a hot coffee between our knees.

We can do all of those extra things because the job of driving has been handed over to the unconscious mind who, by the way, is far better at that kind of thing than we are! And it's at this point that we know we have moved to level 4.

Unconscious Competence. (I'm in flow and this is easy!)

Reaching this point is like reaching the pot of gold at the end of the rainbow. It's the Nirvana of your learning journey. This is the moment in which *you don't know that you know*. You just do! Spanish literally pours out from your mouth without having to think about it. You realise you're talking to yourself in your mind in Spanish. You may even dream in Spanish.

When you speak, it seems effortless and you focus more on 'what' you want to say rather than 'how' to say it. It's this level that every student of the Spanish language wants to reach.

It is at this level that you say things you didn't know that you knew. Words just pop out of your mouth, unplanned and more surprisingly, they are correct! This is a great place to be and getting here requires one thing and one thing alone. It's no secret and it certainly isn't one of those shortcut, 'learn Spanish in a weekend' systems.

To get here all you need to do is repeatedly practice speaking a very correct Spanish over and over and over again until it is accepted with open arms into your unconscious mind. (The unconscious will accept bad Spanish just as readily.)

Warning: These levels of learning are by no means a one-way street. Moving through them could be likened to playing a game of 'Snakes and Ladders'. Every new realisation, learning or piece of information that comes your way can whiz you back through the levels in a matter of seconds.

Not only that, but you can be at different levels with different concepts. Perhaps you are in level 4 in the present and the future and use them fluently. Yet, when it comes to speaking in the past you drop back to level 3 or even to level 2.

Perhaps you command the majority of your Spanish at level 4 but when it comes to the subjunctive you drop right back. All this can happen quickly and is something that often disappoints us terribly. Yet, you needn't be upset. It's completely normal. This is how the mind works.

The great news: Once you have reached level 4, when some new information takes you back down through the levels, you will find that you quickly rebound back up faster and faster. And each time with more confidence than before!

Another way of looking at this is that, at the beginning, learning Spanish is like trying to build a 10,000 piece jig-saw puzzle. The problem you have, however, is that the box-top is missing and you don't know what picture it is that you're trying to piece together.

That's why everything is so slow at the beginning. You have all these pieces with absolutely no idea of where to start placing them.

However, by the time you've got the corners in place, the edges done and most of the middle filled in, then it's a very different story. We now know that when a person, a book, a podcast or a webpage gives us a new piece of information, we have to drop down a few levels whilst we look for where that piece fits into the puzzle.

And, even though that happens, because so much of the picture is already created, it takes very little effort to find the right place for it in your mind. And, once that's done, you quickly bounce back to where you were. What's more, the more this happens, the less of a puzzle it becomes, as your Spanish converts into a beautiful work of art!

You can be patient with yourself.

No matter how smart you imagine you should be, until they find a way of downloading languages into our brains by some other means (Gulp! We'd be out of a job.) you will have to resign yourself to the aforementioned system.

Now that you know how it works, however, you can be more patient with yourself. You are just like everyone else and you have to pass through the learning levels like everyone else. Be aware that level three is the place where you will spend the majority of your time. And that's great.

It's in level three that all the good work is done. By studying good information, practising frequently and learning on a daily basis you are preparing the information for its transfer to the unconscious part of your mind.

Believe us when we say that you really don't need to rush this level. Once the information moves into the unconscious mind and to level 4 it becomes part of what we call 'our habits' and the last thing you want to do is install bad habits in Spanish. (We all know how hard it can be to change a habit.)

So, be patient with yourself and accept any set backs for what they are; simply new pieces of information that will ultimately enhance your Spanish. Accept confusion as a vital part of your learning and give yourself a break when you say the wrong things or make mistakes. It's all part of the learning process and it won't last forever.

Oh, and above all else, enjoy the journey. It can really be fun!

Now, talking about fun, you've had enough of a break to be ready to launch into the next major part of your Subjunctive learning journey... the Imperfect Subjunctive!

The Imperfect Subjunctive.

So far you have only worked with examples that came from the Present Subjunctive. Now we are going to turn toward what the grammar books call the Imperfect Subjunctive, but what we prefer to call the PAST Subjunctive.

Why? Basically because when we make the same sentences in the past as we have been making in the present or future, we have to use the Imperfect/Past Subjunctive.

You will notice in this section that the exercises are shorter. This is because you have already practised the triggers in the Present Subjunctive portion of the book. As you will see, although the verb conjugation is different, the way the Imperfect subjunctive is triggered off is identical to what you have practiced already.

Regular Verbs

Before we get into the process of using the Past Subjunctive, let's take a look at how it's constructed. Interestingly, you have two types of endings that you can choose from. Both are correct and one isn't better than another. Some statistics show that the ARA/IERA version is more popular than the ASE/IESE version, but you can choose the one that is easier for you to use and to remember.

Take a look at the two ways of conjugating a regular AR verb in the Past Subjunctive. As always, we use the VERB STEM as the root of the conjugation.

In this example using HABLAR, the verb stem is HABL. We have highlighted the endings that you have to add each time.

HABLAR = TO DO

Yo	habl**ara**	Nosotros	habl**áramos**
Tú	habl**aras**	Vosotros	habl**arais**
Él Ella Usted	habl**ara**	Ellos Ellas Ustedes	habl**aran**

or

Yo	habl**ase**	Nosotros	habl**ásemos**
Tú	habl**ases**	Vosotros	habl**aseis**
Él Ella Usted	habl**ase**	Ellos Ellas Ustedes	habl**asen**

Then, we have another two options for ER/IR verbs. Whatever you do for ER verbs, you do for IR verbs, too. They break down like this:

COMER = TO DO

Yo	com**iera**	Nosotros	com**iéramos**
Tú	com**ieras**	Vosotros	com**ierais**
Él Ella } Usted	com**iera**	Ellos Ellas } Ustedes	com**ieran**

or

Yo	com**iese**	Nosotros	com**iésemos**
Tú	com**ieses**	Vosotros	com**ieseis**
Él Ella } Usted	com**iese**	Ellos Ellas } Ustedes	com**iesen**

Irregular Verbs

There are plenty irregular verbs in the Imperfect/Past Subjunctive tense. However, it's easy to know when they are irregular and how to conjugate them.

At the level you are at now, you will undoubtedly be familiar with the Preterite tense or the Simple Past (I ate, you went, she spoke.)

All of the verbs that are irregular in the Preterite tense are irregular in the Imperfect Subjunctive, too.

166

To know how to conjugate the Imperfect Subjunctive all you do is to look at the verb stem in the Preterite and bolt the Subjunctive endings onto it.

Here's an example.

TENER.

This is irregular in its preterite form.

It breaks down like this: TUVE, TUVISTE, TUVO etc.

So, the stem is TUV

Taking that stem, TUV, you then add the Imperfect Subjunctive endings:

TENER = TO HAVE

Yo	**TUV**iera	Nosotros	**TUV**iéramos
Tú	**TUV**ieras	Vosotros	**TUV**ierais
Él Ella Usted	**TUV**iera	Ellos Ellas Ustedes	**TUV**ieran

or

Yo	**TUV**iese	Nosotros	**TUV**iésemos
Tú	**TUV**ieses	Vosotros	**TUV**ieseis
Él Ella Usted	**TUV**iese	Ellos Ellas Ustedes	**TUV**iesen

As you can see, the endings are literally dropped onto the irregular preterite verb stem. Have a go at conjugating some of the other irregular verbs:

Exercise 24

PONER = TO PUT

Yo _____   Nosotros _____

Tú _____   Vosotros _____

Él ⎫
Ella ⎬ _____   Ellos ⎫
Usted ⎭   Ellas ⎬ _____
Ustedes ⎭

SABER = TO KNOW

Yo _____   Nosotros _____

Tú _____   Vosotros _____

Él ⎫
Ella ⎬ _____   Ellos ⎫
Usted ⎭   Ellas ⎬ _____
Ustedes ⎭

VENIR = TO COME

Yo _____   Nosotros _____

Tú _____   Vosotros _____

Él ⎫
Ella ⎬ _____   Ellos ⎫
Usted ⎭   Ellas ⎬ _____
Ustedes ⎭

Verbs like DECIR.

When 'decir' is conjugated in the Preterite, its stem changes to DIJ. For example: Dije, dijiste, dijo, dijimos dijisteis, dijeron.

You are probably aware that when the irregular preterite root has a J in it, then the 'J' takes the place of the letter 'I' in the full conjugation.

e.g.

dijeron and not **dijleron**

The same applies to the Imperfect Subjunctive and the J takes the place of the I.

Here are some examples:

CONDUCIR = TO DRIVE

Yo	**conduj**era	Nosotros	**conduj**éramos
Tú	**conduj**eras	Vosotros	**conduj**erais
Él Ella Usted	}**conduj**era	Ellos Ellas Ustedes	} **conduj**eran

TRADUCIR = TO TRANSLATE

Yo	**traduj**era	Nosotros	**traduj**éramos
Tú	**traduj**eras	Vosotros	**traduj**erais
Él Ella Usted	}**traduj**era	Ellos Ellas Ustedes	} **traduj**eran

Just before we launch into the mechanics of how to put all these verbs into action, it's worth looking at how two of the most irregular verbs: SER and IR. Like in the Preterite, they share the same conjugation in the Imperfect Subjunctive.

IR/SER = TO GO/BE

Yo	fuera/se	Nosotros	fuéramos/semos
Tú	fueras/ses	Vosotros	fuerais/seis
Él		Ellos	
Ella }	fuera/se	Ellas }	fueran/sen
Usted		Ustedes	

And...now to the Nitty Gritty.

So, now that we know how to conjugate the verbs, it's time to start to look at how they are used in sentences.

The great news is that there is little new information here. The reason for that is that the triggers are all the same. The only difference is that they are all set in the past tense, rather than the present or the future.

Let's start with **Wishes.** O.O.P.A.

The Trigger structure is like this:

wish/hope + QUE + subjunctive

esperar que ...
to wish/ hope/ expect that ...

ojalá que ...
if only/I wish ...

esperar a que...
to wait for…

The first Wishes trigger we started with was:

Ojalá que... = If only/I wish...

However, we are going to leave 'ojalá que...' until a little later for reasons that will become clear when we get to it. This Trigger has two jobs when used with the Imperfect/Past Subjunctive and so we need to look at those separately.

For the moment we will start with the next Wish Trigger:

Esperar = To hope/expect/wait

This trigger works in the past just as it does in the present. The only difference is that when the Trigger is fired in the past, then the past subjunctive is used. Here are some examples:

I was waiting for him to arrive.

Esperaba a **que** él **llegara/ase.**

171

I hoped that he knew the combination to the safe.

Esperaba que supiera/iese él la combinación de la caja fuerte.

The man expected to win the lottery soon.

El hombre **esperaba que** le **tocara/ase** la lotería pronto.

So, as you have probably noticed, the format and structure is identical to the one we used in the present tense except that this time we use the past tense words.

Preterite or Imperfect Past?

The extra consideration that you have in the past, of course, is the choice of whether you should use the Preterite or Imperfect for your trigger.

This book isn't about that particular grammatical issue and so, if you find that you are choosing Preterite when we are using Imperfect or visa versa, don't worry too much about it. Most times you will be correct anyway. If you are unsure, perhaps it would be worth visiting our website at **www.lightspeedspanish.co.uk** and looking at some of the podcasts we have on these grammar points in 'El Aula'.

A Tip for Managing the Imperfect Past

Just as a rule of thumb, however, watch out for sentences that have 'was...ing' or 'were...ing' in them, or 'used to'. It's very likely that they will be imperfect.

For example:

She **was** wait**ing** for the boys to call.

Ella **esperaba** a que llamaran/asen los chicos.

Equally this sentence could use the continuous past:

Ella **estaba esperando** a que...

Both are correct and you can choose the one you prefer.

And of course, if you are using a 'used to' sentence, you will use the regular Imperfect Past.

For example:

The two old men always **used to** wait on the corner for their friend to appear.

Los dos hombres mayores siempre **esperaban** en la esquina a que apareciera/iese su amigo.

Preterite Past

Likewise, if there is a real sense of measurement in the sentence, then it's very likely that you will use the Preterite Past. For example:

He waited **for three hours** for the postman/mailman to arrive.

Él **esperó** tres horas a que llegara/ase el cartero.

Ahora te toca a ti.

Ahora vamos a practicar el Imperfecto de Subjuntivo con el verbo esperar.

Exercise 25

1, The pilot hoped that the passengers were calm during the whole journey.

_____

2, Ana and Alfonso expected that their parents would say something to them about their behaviour.

_____

3, The nun hoped that the priest would allow her to write the next sermon.

_____

4, Alejandro waited for twenty minutes for his teacher to come and talk to him.

_____

5, Cynthia was expecting her exam results to be good.

_____

W.Opinions. O.P.A. in the Imp. Subjunctive

Because we have already covered the triggers for this family in the present, we don't necessarily have to cover all of the options again, (you can flip back if you need to recall some of the triggers) but what we will do is to show examples of some of the main kinds of Opinion triggers when they occur in the past.

If you recall, in the Present Indicative, one important trigger was this:

Es bueno que...

It's good that...

How this works in the past is like this:

It was good that the mayor spoke about the plans for the village this year.

Fue bueno que el alcalde **hablara/ase** de los planes para el pueblo este año.

It was good that my mum told me those things when I was young.

Fue bueno que mi madre me **dijera/ese** esas cosas cuando yo era joven.

¿FUE o ERA?

Once again, this isn't the place to get into the differences between ERA and FUE, however, just as a rule of thumb; one off things tend to be FUE.

If you remember the sentence,

'Ayer **FUE** lunes.'

it can help you to recall that one-off events or actions tend to use the preterite.

Mixing the present and the past.

Here is probably a great time to talk about how, just as you can in English, you can mix some of the present tense triggers with the past in Spanish. Take a look at these examples:

It's very interesting that they didn't vote for the main candidate.

Es muy **interesante que** no **votaran/asen** por el candidato principal.

It's ridiculous that they didn't say sorry to us.

Es ridículo que no nos **pidieran/iesen** perdón.

Note: From this point onwards we will use only the IERA/ARA version in the examples and answers and you can use which ever one you prefer. You may even choose to vary from sentence to sentence.

The QUÉ opinion triggers

Now, let's take a look at the Opinion triggers that start with 'Qué'.

Qué curioso que...

How curious that...

This is how they work in the past:

How curious that the council didn't call us yesterday.

Qué curioso que el ayuntamiento no nos **llamara** ayer.

How horrible that the police did that to them.

Qué horrible que la policía les **hiciera** eso.

¿Ya has cogido la idea? Muy bien. Pues, ahora deberíamos practicarlo un rato.

Ahora te toca a ti.

Exercise 26

1, It's good that Cristina caught her flight.

_____

2, How awesome that Pedro passed his exams.

_____

3, It used to fascinate me that the neighbour never left his house during the day.

_____

4, It annoyed me that I had to wait half an hour alone in his office.

_____

5, It's incredible that I really met Manu Chao.

_____

6, How nice that your boyfriend bought you that for your birthday. (tú)

_____

7, It bothered him that it rained without pause that week.

_____

8, My dad loved it that I was able to get a job in his firm.

_____

9, How frustrating that nobody knew where the wedding was.

_____

10, It's better that it happened like that.

_____

¿Cómo te fueron estas frases? ¿Ya entiendes un poco más?

Momento de Repaso.

So, what we have seen here is that you can use the triggers in the past when talking about past events. What is more, you can use some of the triggers in the present, to talk about past events, too.

So, now you know that, we will intersperse the variations in all of the forthcoming exercises.

W.O. **Obligations**.P.A in the Imp. Subj.

Now let's take a look at how this works with the Obligations family of triggers.

Here's a typical trigger:

Querer que...
To want that...

And, now, let's look at how this would work in the past:

My father wanted me to be home for ten-thirty.

Mi padre **quiso que estuviera** en casa para las diez y media.

His mother wanted him to be a fireman.

Su madre **quería que fuera** bombero.

Interestingly, because of their structure, the Obligation family of Triggers doesn't lend itself very easily to mixing the present and the past together. So, if you are referring to the past, with Obligation, the trigger will tend to be in the past also.

So, are you ready for a test?

¡Vamos!

Ahora te toca a ti.

Exercise 27

1, The landlord always preferred that I paid the rent at the end of the month.

_____

2, The shop assistant asked me to show her my identification.

_____

3, It was important that Mercedes took her tablets each hour.

_____

4, It was preferable that the guests didn't go into that room.

_____

5, There was no need for your mother to say that to you. (tú)

_____

6, The captain insisted that his team ate a light lunch before the game.

_____

7, The waiter recommended that we tried the Spanish omelette.

_____

8, It was advisable that everyone took a coat with them.

_____

9, The people there suggested that we caught the next bus to Madrid.

_____

10, It was unnecessary for so many people to die during the First World War.

_____

¿Qué tal? ¿Sacaste buenas notas?

You've probably noticed that we are fairly whizzing you through the past tense examples. The reason for this is that, apart from the different conjugation, the structure is identical to what you have been practicing in the present.

However, this isn't all there is to the Imperfect/Past Subjunctive. There are other structures that we need to cover, too, as we move forward.

Then, once we have all of that under our belt we will making things a little more complicated by mixing all of the triggers in the past and present together.

W.O.O.**Possibilities.A** in the Imp.Subj.

Okay. Now it's time to look at how we use the past tense with this family of triggers. Let's see how they work. Here are a few examples:

No pensar que...	**Es posible que...**
To not think that...	It's possible that...
No es verdad que...	**¿Tener algo que...?**
It's not true that...	To have something that...?

Look how they work in the past:

Milvia didn't think that the result was fair.

Milvia **no pensó que** el resultado **fuera** justo.

This one could just as easily work as a mix of present and past:

Milvia doesn't think that the decision was fair.

Milvia **no piensa que** el resultado **fuera** justo.

It was possible that the cowboys lived like that.

Era posible que los vaqueros **vivieran** así.

or

It is possible that the cowboys lived like that.

Es posible que los vaqueros **vivieran** así.

¿Has capturado la idea? Pues ¿practicamos un poco?

Ahora te toca.

Exercise 28

1, It's probable that the ship sank in that area.

_____

2, The surgeon didn't believe that the patient had a serious problem.

_____

3, I very much doubt that the grandchildren did that on purpose.

_____

4, The stranger wanted to know if there was anyone who was able to help him.

_____

5, So, didn't you have anything that was strong enough to hold it? (ustedes)

_____

6, The president wasn't saying that he was going to fix the problems easily.

_____

7, There was nothing we could do that would make him happy again.

———————————————————————————

8, Maybe the prime minister knew something that we didn't.

———————————————————————————

9, The identical twins deny that they were involved.

———————————————————————————

10, At that moment I didn't know anyone who spoke Spanish.

———————————————————————————

¿Cómo vas con todo esto? ¿Crees que ya tienes la idea de cómo funciona el Imperfecto de Subjuntivo?

Really, the more you do these exercises the more you are probably noticing that what you do in the present, you also do in the past. The only difference is that you use the past subjunctive. The triggers are the same and they trigger in the past just as they do in the future.

In the present you can have sentences with two or more subjunctives in them. In the past, too. You can see that in question 7 above.

In addition to that, the extra skill you have now is that you can mix the time frames of the present and the past and still control the use of the subjunctive.

¡Eres una máquina!

Now, let's take a look at how the past subjunctive works with the last of the Subjunctive groups, the Afterwards family.

W.O.O.P.**Afterwards** in the Imp.Subj.

Let's look at some examples of how these triggers work in the past:

All the family members had to get their coats before leaving to have a walk.

Todos los miembros de la familia tuvieron que coger sus abrigos **antes de que salieran** a dar un paseo.
('antes de salir' is also possible.)

The chef added salt so that the food had more flavour.

El chef añadió sal **para que** la comida **tuviera** más sabor.

The boy's mum wanted him to call her when he arrived.

La madre del chico quería que la **llamara en cuanto llegara**.

Have you noticed that the last example contains two triggers? The first one is an Obligation trigger and the second is an Afterward trigger. This is also quite normal.

As your Spanish progresses, the more you find yourself firing off multiple triggers. This is because our conversation becomes so diverse that we combine many structures in the one sentence.

This is where you will get to (if you are not there already)!

Ahora te toca a ti.

Let's practice our Afterwards triggers in the past.

Exercise 29

1, Father said that as long as I got good grades, I could go skiing in Italy.

_____

2, The man was going to work until it became dark.

_____

3, Spain changed a lot after the Moors arrived there.

_____

4, The chef added more cream so the food would taste better.

_____

5, We were going to look for Elizabeth as soon as the others arrived.

_____

¿Cómo te han ido estas frases? Esperamos que te fueran bien.

Repaso.

Now, as we draw to the close of this part of the Past/Imperfect Subjunctive, we think it's a good time to test your ability to identify non-triggers, extended triggers, double triggers and multiple triggers. This should be a challenging exercise, so 'prepárate'. Buena suerte☺

Exercise 30

1, We hoped that our friends would tell us about the birth as soon as they knew.

_____

_____

2, It was curious that Juan, the neighbour's son who goes to the same school as my son, didn't arrive on time yesterday.

_____

_____

3, I used to believe that it wasn't possible that they could do such terrible things.

_____

_____

4, I thought the girls weren't going to come until three.

_____

_____

5, I didn't know if the neighbours knew that we were moving to Spain.

_____

_____

6, Pedro and María hoped that the train wouldn't arrive before they bought their tickets.

_____

_____

7, I didn't doubt that the man was telling the truth but I wasn't sure that he knew the whole story.

_____

_____

8, Guillermo thinks that his brother didn't want him to go with him so that he could do something naughty.

_____

_____

9, Maribel wasn't saying that she needed her things by the next day, but that it was important that she had them that week.

_____

_____

10, José María didn't like that Ernesto, whose daughter was dating his son, was telling them what they could and couldn't do.

_____

_____

Y esta vez, ¿cómo te ha ido este ejercicio? Ya se ponen un poco más duros, ¿verdad?

Fear not! With practice, practice and more practice all of these structures that at the moment may seem strange and clumsy will just begin to flow as easily as you can say: antidisestablishmentarianism. :)

Using the Perfect Tense with the Past Subjunctive.

Just as we saw in the present tense, the verb HABER also has its use when forming the past subjunctive. The structure is basically the same as we practised with the present subjunctive, only this time the sentences refer to the past and the 'Have' changes to 'Had'.

Before we start to look at how this works, let's take a look at how HABER conjugates in the Imperfect/Past subjunctive:

HABER

Yo	**HUB**iera	Nosotros	**HUB**iéramos
Tú	**HUB**ieras	Vosotros	**HUB**ierais
Él Ella Usted	**HUB**iera	Ellos Ellas Ustedes	**HUB**ieran

Yo	**HUB**iese	Nosotros	**HUB**iésemos
Tú	**HUB**ieses	Vosotros	**HUB**ieseis
Él Ella Usted	**HUB**iese	Ellos Ellas Ustedes	**HUB**iesen

Here are some examples of how this is used in sentences:

No creía que le **hubiera** dado la información a ese hombre.
I didn't believe that he had given the information to that man.

Fue rarísimo que los obreros **hubieran** terminado tan temprano.
It was really strange that the workers had finished so early.

El cura **esperaba que** a la congregación le **hubiera** gustado el sermón.
The priest hoped that the congregation had liked the sermon.

So, as you can see, the structure is fairly straightforward:

PAST TENSE TRIGGER + HUBIERA + PAST PARTICIPLE

Equally, just as we saw with the exercises where we had a mix of a present tense trigger and a past tense subjunctive, we can have the same situation with Haber. Clearly, this can only apply to the triggers that lend themselves to this kind of structure.

Take a look at these examples:

Es curioso que la jefa **hubiera** salido tan de prisa.
It's strange that the boss had left in such a hurry.

Es muy **posible que** no **hubieran** sabido nada sobre el asunto.
It's very possible that they hadn't known anything about the affair.

Mi padre **no cree que** nos **hubiéramos** quedado en tu casa toda la noche.
My father doesn't believe that we had stayed in your house all night.

Perhaps you've noticed that these sentences are constructed very much as we make them in English. When we use the HAD in English, we use it in Spanish. However, the only extra consideration is whether we have triggered off the subjunctive along the way.

Shall we practise some of these kind of structures?

Ahora te toca a ti.

Exercise 31

1, How interesting that the team had known that all of the time.

_____

2, The photographer hoped that his photos had come out well.

_____

3, We were all going to stay out until we found the ball.

_____

4, I didn't doubt that Ricardo had done a fabulous job.

5, We all agreed that when we had finished painting we would go to the bar.

6, The nurse didn't want to say anything in case someone had already told her

---

7, It was good that Pedro had organised his own party.

8, It was interesting that no one had realised the time.

9, It's doubtful that anyone had know about the problems beforehand.

10, It's not true that the neighbour had been here earlier that day.

¿Cómo te han ido estas frases? Intentamos hacer que sean cada vez más complejas (para que no te aburras, jeje).

Before we move on, it's time to work on our 'power of three' system and review all of the exercises from this portion of the book.

We'll give you them in random order and we ask you to really do them. We know you may be gushing to get on to the next new structure and that's normal, however, by taking time to reinforce your learning, you will emerge from this experience so much more confident and able.

A clever person once said:

"I always do things three times. When I do it for the first time I'm just deciding if I like it or not. When I'm doing it for the second time I'm just kind of getting the hang of it, but it's not easy. When I do it for the third time, I can actually start having fun, and that's what it's all about."

So, here we go. Pónte el cinturón de seguridad...y ¡a por ello!

Exercise 20

1, The dog likes its owners to spend time with him, walk him every day and give him good food.

_____

_____

2, María thinks that it is strange that her boyfriend doesn't call and doesn't visit her as much as before.

_____

_____

3, As soon as I finish painting and making the dinner, I'll go to pick you up. (tú)

_____

_____

4, It's possible that the boys are in their class now and can't answer their phones.

_____

_____

Exercise 26

1, It's good that Cristina caught her flight.

_____

2, How awesome that Pedro passed his exams.

_____

3, It used to fascinate me that the neighbour never left his house during the day.

_____

4, It annoyed me that I had to wait half an hour alone in his office.

_____

5, It's incredible that I really met Manu Chao.

6, How nice that your boyfriend bought you that for your birthday. (tú)

7, It bothered him that it rained without pause that week.

8, My dad loved it that I was able to get a job in his firm.

9, How frustrating that nobody knew where the wedding was.

10, It's better that it happened like that.

Exercise 23

1, How awesome that the team have won for the third time.

2, Unless Elena has written it herself, I can't accept it.

3, It interests Guillermo that all of his friends have grown beards. (dejarse crecer)

_____

4, My parents-in-law love that they have been able to see their grandson every day.

_____

5, The politician denies that he has been involved in the dirty business of accepting bribes.

_____

6, Leticia doubts that her husband has remembered her birthday.

_____

7, It's better that you have spoken with Diego before he leaves for Paris. (tú)

_____

8, Cristina prefers that the dogs have had their walk before nine o'clock.

_____

9, Mari Carmen says that it's important that all of the people have arrived by twelve.

_____

10, The logical thing is that you have seen the papers before the lawyer arrives. (ustedes)

_____

Exercise 28

1, It's probable that the ship sank in that area.

_____

2, The surgeon didn't believe that the patient had a serious problem.

_____

3, I very much doubt that the grandchildren did that on purpose.

_____

4, The stranger wanted to know if there was anyone who was able to help him.

_____

5, So, didn't you have anything that was strong enough to hold it? (ustedes)

_____

6, The president wasn't saying that he was going to fix the problems easily.

_____

7, There was nothing we could do that would make him happy again.

_____

8, Maybe the prime minister knew something that we didn't.

_____

9, The identical twins deny that they were involved.

_____

10, At that moment I didn't know anyone who spoke Spanish.

_____

Exercise 21

1, Unless they tell you, you can always ask them to give you an extra day. (tú)

_____

_____

2, After we arrive do you want us to do anything in particular? (usted)

_____

_____

3, How frustrating that they don't want us to be there tomorrow. *

_____

4, It's ridiculous that we pay so many taxes when all we need is that they provide the basic services.

_____

_____

5, The fascinating thing is that we can choose whatever we like.

_____

_____

Exercise 29

1, Father said that as long as I got good grades, I could go skiing in Italy.

_____

2, The man was going to work until it became dark.

_____

3, Spain changed a lot after the Moors arrived there.

4, The chef added more cream so the food would taste better.

5, We were going to look for Elizabeth as soon as the others arrived.

Exercise 27

1, The landlord always preferred that I paid the rent at the end of the month.

2, The shop assistant asked me to show her my identification.

3, It was important that Mercedes took her tablets each hour.

4, It was preferable that the guests didn't go into that room.

5, There was no need for your mother to say that to you. (tú)

_____

6, The captain insisted that his team ate a light lunch before the game.

_____

7, The waiter recommended that we tried the Spanish omelette.

_____

8, It was advisable that everyone took a coat with them.

_____

9, The people there suggested that we caught the next bus to Madrid.

_____

10, It was unnecessary for so many people to die during the First World War.

_____

Exercise 22.

1, It's advisable that the head teacher prohibits that the students use mobiles in the classroom.

_____

_____

2, How terrible that the partners are saying that the investors must withdraw their money.

_____

_____

3, As long as it is important that we know that information, we should learn it well.

_____

_____

Exercise 31

1, How interesting that the team had known that all of the time.

_____

2, The photographer hoped that his photos had come out well.

_____

3, We were all going to stay out until we found the ball.

_____

4, I didn't doubt that Ricardo had done a fabulous job.

_____

5, We all agreed that when we had finished painting we would go to the bar.

6, The nurse didn't want to say anything in case someone had already told her

---

7, It was good that Pedro had organised his own party.

8, It was interesting that no one had realised the time.

9, It's doubtful that anyone had know about the problems beforehand.

10, It's not true that the neighbour had been here earlier that day.

Exercise 25

1, The pilot hoped that the passengers were calm during the whole journey.

2, Ana and Alfonso expected that their parents would say something to them about their behaviour.

_____

3, The nun hoped that the priest would allow her to write the next sermon.

_____

4, Alejandro waited for twenty minutes for his teacher to come and talk to him.

_____

5, Cynthia was expecting her exam results to be good.

_____

Exercise 30

1, We hoped that our friends would tell us about the birth as soon as they knew.

_____

_____

2, It was curious that Juan, the neighbour's son who goes to the same school as my son, didn't arrive on time yesterday.

_____

_____

3, I used to believe that it wasn't possible that they could do such terrible things.

_____

_____

4, I thought the girls weren't coming until three.

_____

_____

5, I didn't know if the neighbours knew that we were moving to Spain.

_____

_____

6, Pedro and María hoped that the train wouldn't arrive before they bought their tickets.

_____

_____

7, I didn't doubt that the man was telling the truth but I wasn't sure that he knew the whole story.

_____

_____

8, Guillermo thinks that his brother didn't want him to go with him so that he could do something naughty.

_____

_____

9, Maribel wasn't saying that she needed her things by the next day, but that it was important that she had them that week.

_____

_____

10, José María didn't like that Ernesto, whose daughter was dating his son, was telling them what they could and couldn't do.

_____

_____

¡Vaya maratón!, ¿verdad? Ahora, ¿cómo te sientes en cuanto a todo esto? ¿Más cómodo/a? ¿Más seguro/a de ti mismo/a? Para ahora deberías tener mucha más confianza porque la práctica te hace perfecto/a.

¡Enhorabuena!

You can be very proud of yourself now for having completed the biggest and most complex part of learning the Imperfect/Past Subjunctive. That's it! It's done!

However, if you took note of the flowchart at the beginning of the book you'll know that we haven't quite got to the glass of Cava yet.

There are still some very important structures that we must address in order for you to have a well rounded knowledge of how the subjunctive is used.

So, let's carry on moving forward.

The Famous IF-WOULD structure.

As you may recall from the beginning of the book, I said that there were two lovely people who helped me to have a light bulb moment regarding the Subjunctive in English. One was Peter Løvstrøm who showed me how we use the present subjunctive in our language and the other was Cynthia, the co-creator of LightSpeed Spanish. (¡Gracias, mi amor!).

What I never realised was that just as we have the Present Subjunctive in English, we also have the Past Subjunctive. What's more, it's very easy to identify, something that will help us massively in this portion of the book.

However, before we get to that we had better discuss the structure a little. This is what we call the IF-WOULD structure and is used as much in English as it is in Spanish.

The most important part.

What we would like you to keep in mind is that this structure has nothing to do with anything that we have discussed so far.

It will be far easier for you to look at it as a wholly independent part of the Spanish language. It uses the Past Subjunctive but it really isn't at all linked to the triggers we have seen up to now.

In fact, it has a trigger all of its own, which helps you to keep from mixing it up with other similar kinds of sentences that do NOT use the Subjunctive.

Take a look at this sentence for example:

If I **won** the lottery I **would** move to Spain.

Si **ganara** la lotería me **mudaría** a España.

This sentence is the typical IF-WOULD structure that is used in both English and Spanish.

So, because we use these kind of sentences without giving them much thought, we aren't aware of just how unusual they are. And it was Cynthia who brought this strangeness to my attention.

One day she asked me to tell her what time frame this kind of sentence was referring to; was it the past, present or future?

I said, as you would too, that it was talking about a future possibility, so therefore, it was set in the future.

"Exactly!" she said. "Why then", she asked, "does it say: 'If I **won** the lottery' and not: 'If I **win** the lottery'?"

And that was my light bulb moment. I realised that the English **Imperfect Subjunctive** in this kind of structure is a **past tense** verb that talks about a **future** event!

I had never picked up on that before! What's more, I felt quite stupid that someone who wasn't even a native English speaker was teaching me about my own language!

What I realise now is that one of the issues we have as native speakers is that we become blind to our own language. We don't see the anomalies in it because, for us, they sound correct and so we don't question them.

Living with a non-native speaker has been a real eye opener for me. I have discovered lots of curiosities about my own language simply because Cynthia has the ability to be far more objective than I ever could be. (Like when she asked me why we can say in English: It's five past one. Yet we can't say: It's three past one. We have to add the word 'minutes'.)

So, getting back to the theme of this portion, the IF-WOULD structure is easily identified because of two things:

1, It uses a past tense verb to refer to the future.

2, It also includes a 'would/should/could' word.

To better highlight this, let's look at the following two sentences.

1. If they **come** today, we **will** go to the park.

2. If they **came** today, we **would** go to the park.

In sentence 1 we can see that the verb is in **PRESENT** and that it is followed by a **WILL** statement.

Sentence 1 is **NOT** a subjunctive sentence.

Sentence 2, however, has a verb in the **PAST** tense which is followed by a **WOULD** statement.

Sentence 2 **IS** a Imperfect/past subjunctive sentence.

Let's see how they would be structured in Spanish:

1. Si **vienen** mañana, nos **iremos** al parque.

2, Si **vinieran** mañana, nos **iríamos** al parque.

Can you see the difference between the two sentences?

The real question is, however:

What is the difference in meaning between the two sentences?

Meaning is always subjective and it varies from person to person. However, in general, sentence 1 has a more definite feel to it. The message is that there's a high chance of them coming. What's more, the implication is that they're planning to come.

Sentence 2 implies that the event probably isn't going to happen. A more complete sentence is like this: 'If they came we would go to the park (but they're probably not coming so we won't).

It's very important that you grasp this concept. The reason we say that is because once you have it you will know which kind of sentence you should use to communicate exactly what you mean.

Take a look at this other example:

Friend 1: You never call me anymore.

Amiga 1: Ya no me llamas más.

Friend 2: **If** you pick up my call, **I'll call** you today.

Amigo 2: **Si coges/contestas a** mi llamada te **llamaré** hoy.

In this example it's likely that if friend 1 picks up the call she WILL talk with friend 2. Friend 2 is offering to call , all friend 1 needs to do is to answer his call.

Now look at this example:

Friend 1: You never call me anymore.

Amiga 1: Ya no me llamas más.

Friend 2: **If** you **picked** up my calls, I **would** call you.

Amigo 2: **Si cogieras/contestaras a** mis llamadas te **llamaría**.

In this example, friend 2 is kind of implying that the reason they don't call is because friend 1 doesn't pick up. There is no plan to call, rather it's the reason why the call doesn't happen.

So, in essence, the first sentence of IF-WILL is a proactive, 'let's do it' kind of message.

The second sentence of IF-WOULD either explains why something doesn't happen or it places the condition on what would have to be done for it to happen.

So, what do you think? Are you seeing the differences clearly? Are they starting to click into place? Have you got a grasp of what we are driving at?

¿Sí?

Great. Then let's practise them.

Ahora te toca a ti.

Exercise 32

1, If I could, I would buy you a diamond ring.(usted)

_____

2, If you had a million Euros, what would you do?(tú)

_____

3, If they spoke to the man responsible, do you think he would admit to it? (tú)

_____

_____

4, If your girlfriend pays for the ticket, will she go?(tú)

_____

5, If you paid would she go? (ustedes)

_____

6. If I were you, I would tell him as soon as possible. (vosotros/ustedes)

_____

7, If it comes today, where will you put the vase? (tú)

_____

8, If we leave this afternoon, we'll be there by tomorrow.

_____

9, If the doctor told you that, then you would have to do it. (usted)

_____

10, If the doctor tells you that, will you do it? (tú)

_____

¿Ya? ¿Todo bien?

Don't worry if this concept seems a little blurry, it will become more clear as you move on.

IF/WILL in the past.

Let's look now at how the IF/WILL sentences work in the past. Just as the present tense IF/WILL structure doesn't need the Subjunctive, so the past tense structure doesn't use it either.

In the past, however, the IF/WILL changes to IF/PAST TENSE.

Let's make this a little clearer for you.

Take a look at how the NON subjunctive IF works in the past.

If she **though**t she could treat me that way she **was** totally mistaken.

Si pensaba que me podía tratar así, **estaba** totalmente equivocada.

It's with this structure that you have to box-clever a little. The reason is that if you just registered the IF and the past tense verb following it, you would immediately decide that it was the IF/WOULD structure.

However, can you notice that there is no 'would' in this sentence? It's **missing the last trigger** and so does **NOT** require the subjunctive.

Let's talk turkey here.

We are going to practise some examples of these kinds of sentences in a moment, however, we really don't want you to get confused over this, so our advice is that if this part feels overwhelming or unclear just leave it for now and you can come back to it later.

What we have done is to highlight it for you so that you can start to identify these structures when you read or listen to people speaking.

Hearing and seeing it used will help to put it into the correct place in your mind. In particular, listen out for when you say something like this in English.

So, let's practise a few sentences.

Ahora te toca a ti.

Exercise 33

1, If you had a friend there I didn't see her. (tú)

_____

2, If he ate the whole pie, I didn't know anything about it.

_____

3, If they were going to send me it, it never arrived.

_____

4, If they thought they could do that then they didn't count on me.

_____

_____

5, If you gave me the keys I don't know where I put them. (tú)

_____

¿Cómo te ha ido este ejercicio? ¿Tiene sentido este tipo de estructura?

As we have said, it's important to know that these kind of sentences can be made, but they aren't something that you should get too hung up on for the moment.

The whole process that is being presented in this book is very broad (as you may have noticed) and there are many things for you to take in. So, be kind to yourself and if you feel overwhelmed by the volume of information, just take a break and come back to it.

It's amazing how distracting your mind with another activity or having a well deserved nap can give you a completely new perspective on things.

The Conditional + QUE + Past Subjunctive

Another structure that is closely linked to the IF/WOULD sentences is the one that uses the conditional with QUE. Once again, as you look at the examples, perhaps you can see just how similar they are to what you have just seen in the IF/WOULD section:

Sería fenomenal **que tuviéramos** otro bebé.

It would be wonderful that we had another baby.

Me **gustaría que** me **escucharas** un poco más.

I would like you to listen to me a little more.

Para **que supiéramos** la verdad **tendría** que ocurrir un milagro.

For us to know the truth there would have to be a miracle.

Can you notice that it's as if the QUE were taking the place of SI? Basically that is the only difference between the two structures.

What's more, just like in the other construction, the sentences can be switched around but the shape still stays the same.

Let's try some sentences now and practice this a little.

Ahora te toca.

Exercise 33a

1, It could be possible that I'm learning this well.

_____

2, I'd like it to be true.

_____

3, Would you want me to do that now. (tú)

_____

4, For there to be a better atmosphere we would need to talk.

_____

5, I wouldn't want you to feel bad about what happened. (Usted)

_____

¿Ya? ¿lo ves? ¡Maravilloso!

Now, let's look at something else that is very much linked to what we are looking at now.

The two jobs of Ojalá with the imperfect/Past subjunctive.

Way back in the book we said we would come back to look at the use of 'Ojalá' with the past subjunctive and this seems like a good time to do so.

We wanted to leave this trigger until you had practised the IF/WOULD structure.

The reason for that is that this trigger has two jobs and one of them is similar to IF/WOULD.

Job number one:

Job one is to wish for things in the future just as we do with the IF/WOULD structure, only this time we are saying 'I wish' or 'If only'. Interestingly, when 'Ojalá' is used with the imperfect/past subjunctive, the QUE is dropped.

Take a look at these examples:

Ojalá tuviera un poco más de dinero (porque así podría comprármelo).*

I wish I had a little bit more money (because that way I could buy myself it).

Ojalá llegara Juan con una pizza y una botella de champán. (Eso sería maravilloso.)*

If only Juan **would come** with a pizza and a bottle of champagne. (That would be wonderful.)

(*The sentences can stand on their own perfectly well without the extra information in brackets. We've just added it so that you can compare them with the following sentences.)

As you can see, both of these sentences have the feel of a wish that is very likely not going to happen. What's more, they both refer to a possible future. (Albeit highly unlikely.)

So, you can probably notice that this kind of sentence is almost identical in feel to the IF/WOULD. In fact, the two sentences could be interchangeable:

Look at this:

Si tuviera un poco más de dinero **podría** comprármelo.

If I had a little bit more money I could buy myself it.

Sería maravilloso **si** Juan **viniera** con una pizza y una botella de champán.

It would be wonderful if Juan came with a pizza and a bottle of champagne.

Can you notice how similar the two structures are?

Job number two:

Job two of 'Ojalá' is to allow us to wish for things in the past just as it does in the future.

Just as we have seen with its first job, 'Ojalá' works without the 'que'. In addition to that, when you wish in the past you will be using 'Haber' as there really isn't another way of doing so.

Here are some examples of how it works:

Ojalá me lo **hubiera** dicho antes de la boda.

I wish she had told me it before the wedding.

Ojalá el ejército **hubiera** llegado unos días antes.

If only the army had arrived a few days before.

It's interesting that the root of the word 'ojalá' comes from the Arabic language. (In Arabic it's شاءو الله – wa-šā' allāh).

The Arabic words means 'if Allah wants' or 'if Allah wills' and so that's why there is a 'wish' feel to the word.

So, now that we have seen two jobs it does, why don't we practise using 'ojalá' a little.

Ahora te toca.

Exercise 34

1, I wish the girl in the next office would talk to me.

_____

2 , If only the bank manager had given him the loan.

_____

3, If only my students would study a little bit harder.

_____

4, If only my teacher had taught me how to do it properly.

_____

5, I wish I could see my grandmother just one more time.

_____

6, If only there were more people like you in the world. (tú)

_____

7, If only the lights would work on the car.

_____

8, I wish the show had gone on forever.

_____

9, If only we could talk more by Skype.

_____

10, I wish that Juana had told me how she felt before leaving.

_____

¿Qué tal todo? Suponemos que ya dominas todo esto, ¿no?

A moment of reflection.

Perhaps you can see, what's happening as you make your way through all of these exercises is that, not only are you getting tremendous practice at forming, recognising and using the subjunctive, but also you are becoming very good at making regular day to day sentences.

Maybe you've noticed that the style of the sentences can be quite repetitive, too. (Although that doesn't mean that they are not challenging at times!)

This is because the themes tend to be similar throughout the whole Subjunctive field. What is sure is that by the time we reach the end of this book, you will have written, thought about, puzzled over and created so many successful subjunctive sentences that nothing will faze you again.

Of course, you'll come across new structures that you haven't seen in this book. The difference now, however, will be that you have a framework into which you can place the new combinations.

Yes, you may suffer from the odd bout of Subjunctivitus for a while, but we don't consider that to be terribly bad. Better to be over the top than to sail through your conversations in a tarzanesque way, ignoring the subjunctive like it was going out of fashion.

Something else for you to consider is that by having arrived at this point, you've proven that you have what it takes to really reach the heights of the Spanish language. The fact that you have been focussed or better said, obsessed enough to wade through this amount of information means that your Spanish is going to be exceptional.

Understand that there is a very small band of non-native Spanish speakers who can use the subjunctive consistently well. And you are becoming one of them! Take a moment to enjoy that feeling, now!

So, let's move onwards and upwards with the understanding that you are drawing very close to the end of this book. There remains one more thing to cover in this section and then we move on to the weird and wonderful part of the subjunctive. Then, that will be it! (Then it will be time to go back and start again! jeje)

As if...

Another expression used with the Imperfect/Past subjunctive is the 'as if...' structure.

Look at these examples:

He talks to me **as if** I **were** someone special.

Él me habla **como si fuera** alguien especial.

The F.B.I. arrived **as if** something terrible **had** happened.

El F.B.I. llegó **como si hubiera** pasado algo terrible.

Can you see how this fairly simple structure works? Of all the Past Subjunctive structures, this is probably the most straight forward. Pay special attention to the first example. Did you notice how in English we used the typical 'past tense word' (were) even though we're talking in present tense. Remember that this can be your warning bell to signal the Imperfect/Past Subjunctive.

So, this is how we make this sentence:

Como si + Past Subjunctive

What's more, it's identical to how we say it in English!

Let's practice a few sentences:

Ahora te toca.

Exercise 35

1, Don't talk to me as if I were an idiot! (tú)

_____

2, I'd like you to work as if you were the owner of the business. (usted)

_____

3, Marco arrived tired as if he had had a long day.

_____

4, You are talking as if the world was about to end. (vosotros/ustedes)

_____

5, It's as if it never happened.

_____

Muy bien. Entonces ya hemos terminado la parte normal y corriente del subjuntivo y ahora vamos a empezar a mirar a lo raro o, mejor dicho, a la parte del arte del subjuntivo.

The Weird and the Wonderful.

The QUE trigger.

I personally think that one of the most interesting ways the Subjunctive is used is when the only trigger present is QUE.

We suppose that it's done for speed and efficiency, something that is very common in any language. So with 'QUE', what Spanish speakers are doing is omitting the rest of the trigger. It's still there, it is just unspoken.

This way of shortening for speed is quite common. For example, many students ask why one verb tends to be used over another and the answer is often that the more common verb is the one that is easiest or fastest to say. Take for example Creer and Pensar.

What we've noticed is that most Spanish speakers from Spain say: 'Creo que...' whilst most English speakers of Spanish often use 'Pienso que..'. Both are correct, of course. The case is, however, that 'Creo que...' is simply faster to say and, for that reason, probably tends to be the more common.

Another interesting shortened version of a common sentence is this:

Habérmelo dicho. = You should have told me.

The full version of this sentence should be:

Deberías habérmelo dicho.

However, for speed, they sometimes omit the 'deberías' and just say: 'Have told me it.'

Well, the same applies with the use of the 'QUE' trigger. One of our most favourite films is called, 'Te doy mis ojos.' and is set in Toledo, Spain. In one scene two sisters are talking as they walk along the riverside. One sister is trying to convince the other that she move out of her marital home and live with her. (Did you notice the subjunctive used in this sentence: 'move'?)

The dialogue goes a little like this:

'Que te quedes conmigo un ratito.'

'Que encuentres trabajo aquí.'

'Que te tomes tu tiempo para pensar un poco.'

'A Antonio (her abusive husband) que le den por culo.'

We'll return to the last sentence presently, (jeje) but for the moment let's consider what is happening in these examples.

Basically, the best way to think about all of the above sentences is that they are partly formed. They are partially written triggers with the front end missing.

For example, each of the sentences could quite easily be:

'Es preciso que te quedes conmigo un ratito.'

'Es mejor que encuentres trabajo aquí.'

'Es aconsejable que te tomes tu tiempo para pensar un poco.'

'Quiero que a Antonio (her abusive husband) le den por culo

What happens, however, is that rather than saying the full trigger, many Spanish speakers just start with 'QUE'.

It seems that this way of speaking is rather colloquial, but rest assured, it's used very frequently.

The best way of describing the function of 'QUE' is that it does a similar job to that of the imperative or command tense.

For example:

Que te quedes = Quédate

Que encuentres trabajo = Encuentra trabajo

Que te tomes tu tiempo = Tómate tu tiempo.

So, by using this you are aiming to persuade someone to do something. You'll hear this used far more in spoken Spanish than you will see in written Spanish so listen out for it.

Let's practise this a little. Bear in mind that even though the sentences in the exercise seem to have an imperative structure we would like you to use the 'que' trigger along with the subjunctive.

Also, because this is a very informal style of command using the subjunctive, it's used more between friends and probably should be avoided with 'usted'.

Ahora te toca.

Exercise 36

1, Shut up I'm talking. (tú)

_____

2, Come tomorrow, I'll be there. (tú)

_____

3, Eat the food, if not you'll be hungry later.
(vosotros/ustedes)

_____

4, Don't talk to me like that, you don't have the right. (tú)

_____

5, Be still a moment, I'm trying to put your clothes on. (tú)

_____

¡Comamos! Let's eat.

Have you seen this structure before? The first person, plural ('nosotros') is used in its subjunctive form and it means; 'Let's do something'.

Really, it isn't a subjunctive form but rather an imperative. However, we thought that it would be valuable to mention it since we are talking about the subjunctive used as a command.

Here are some examples:

¿Comemos? Sí, comamos. = Shall we eat? Yes, let's eat.

Hablemos un rato. = Let's talk for a while.

Crucemos aquí. = Let's cross here.

Although this structure is used, it sometimes has a more formal feel to it. Far more common is the use of 'Vamos a...' to say: 'Let's...'

Mira, vamos a hacer esto. = Look, let's do this.

Que te/le/les den...

As promised we are now going to spend a short while looking at this interesting phrase. If you spend any time in Spain you will hear it used in lots of different social settings.

Supposedly, the original expression was this:

'Que te den morcillas.'

It comes from a time when it was common for street dogs to have rabies and the way they would deal with them was to give them a morcilla (black pudding) laced with strychnine to kill them off.

These days, however, the expression has morphed into various others and seemingly the most common is the more brutal:

Que te den por culo. = Go to hell. Shove it up your a@se, Blow it up your a@s.

(And lots of other similar expressions that mean that kind of thing.)

What happens, however, is that normally the entire phrase isn't used. Rather, it's more common to say:

'Que te/le/les den.'

So, when you hear this shortened expression, you can now know that if it is directed toward you, and the tone the person is using isn't playful, then they are upset with you.

Como me digas...

This is another interesting way of using the subjunctive. A Spanish speaker uses this construction to say something like the following:

Como me digas que no, te voy a dar un cachete en el culo.

If you dare to say 'no' to me, I'm going to smack your bottom.

Como él venga aquí con más problemas hoy le voy a decir cuatro verdades.

If he dares to come here today with more problems I'm going to give him a piece of my mind.

Perhaps you have noticed that this use of the subjunctive could quite easily fall into the Afterwards family of triggers as it refers to a possible later event.

With all of these more subtle triggers, we have to be careful not to assume that every time we say: 'como' or 'que' we must use the subjunctive. It all depends on your intention and the context.

Por...

Here we have another interesting construction with 'por' that triggers the subjunctive. This could easily drop itself into the Opinions family.

Take a look at how it is used:

Por muy inteligente que parezca, siempre me ha parecido un poco maleducado.

No matter how intelligent he may seem, he has always seemed a little bit rude to me.

Por difícil que sea, tenemos que terminar todo el trabajo mañana.

No matter how hard it may be, we have to finish all the work tomorrow.

Tips to get out of a 'stuck for words' state.

Like everything, there are many ways to say the same thing. Even if you didn't have this 'por' trigger in your bag of tricks, you could use plenty of others to communicate the above sentence. For example:

Aunque sea difícil...   Even though it may be difficult...

A pesar de que sea difícil... Despite it being difficult...

Quiza sea difícil...   It may be difficult...

Get the idea?

It is worth taking time out to consider this main principle when speaking Spanish.

If you don't know how to say one thing, say something else instead. There is absolutely no need to get stuck or to have to fight with yourself to create the exact same sentence that you had in mind.

Great speakers of any language have the ability to express themselves flexibly. If someone doesn't understand them, then they find another way of saying it.

You can do the same! A great game to play with yourself is to think of something you would want to say in Spanish and then try to find three different ways of saying it.

Try and do this with the following sentence:

Es importante que lleguemos a tiempo.

It's important that we arrive on time.

So, what other things could you say that would communicate this same message?

See if you can come up with three new sentences, then check out some of the options that we offer. If you have something that we don't, great!

Exercise 37

_____

_____

_____

Ahora, después de este descanso, empecemos de nuevo con las formas más raras del subjuntivo.

Siempre y cuando...

This is an interesting structure that once again fits very nicely into the afterwards family of Triggers.

Let's see how this is used in a typical sentence:

Siempre y cuando me hables con respeto, te escucharé.

As long as you talk to me with respect I'll listen to you.

Saldré contigo siempre y cuando me trates bien.

I'll go out with you as long as you treat me nicely.

We like this trigger! Once we have covered more of the strange subjunctive we will practice all of these in our last exercise. After that, it will be review time again. Remember, we still have to review everything one more time to complete our 'power of three' challenge.

Que yo sepa...

This expression is fairly fixed and simply means:

As far as I know.

This is used widely by most native speakers and is used in this way:

Que yo sepa, no han estado aquí en todo el día.

As far as I know they haven't been here all day.

Que yo sepa, no hay ninguna por aquí.

As far as I know, there aren't any around here.

This is the kind of phrase that you don't even have to think about. You just have to remember it and use it like this. Easy! (jaja. Ojalá todo fuera tan simple, ¿verdad?)

Como quieras tú/Como quiera usted.

Here we have a very common usage of the subjunctive which means, 'As you want/wish/ whatever you like.'

It can be used with a very positive tone:

Huesped: ¿Quieres tomar algo?

Host: Do you want to eat/drink something?

Invitado: Sí, gracias. ¿Qué hay?

Guest: Yes, please. What is there?

Huesped: Lo que tú quieras.

Host: Whatever you like.

Equally, it can be used with a more negative tone to show exasperation or frustration.

Marido: No me apetece ir a la fiesta hoy.

Husband: I don't fancy going to the party today.

Mujer: Pero nos invitaron hace mucho.

Wife: But they invited us a good while ago.

Marido: Lo sé, pero no tengo ganas.

Husband: I know, but I can't be bothered.

Mujer: Mira. Tú haz lo que quieras, pero yo me voy vayas tú o no.

Wife: Look. Do what you want but I'm going whether you go or not.

Como tú digas/ Como usted diga.

Just like the previous expression, this is another very common structure used by Spanish speakers which means, 'Whatever you say.'

It is typically used positively in situations in which someone is asking for something and the other person agrees to it.

Jefe: Quiero que se termine el proyecto antes de que usted se vaya de vacaciones.

Boss: I want the project finished before you go on holiday.

Empleado: Como usted diga.

Employee: Whatever you say.

It can, however, like most of these expression, be used in a negative way:

Novia: Quiero que nos casemos en Toledo.

Girlfriend: I want us to get married in Toledo.

Novio: ¿Por qué siempre tenemos que hacerlo como tú digas?

Boyfriend: Why have we always got to do it the way you say?

Sea lo que/cual sea, fuera lo que/cual fuese

These two expressions exist in English too and are used in exactly the same way.

Sea lo que sea = Whatever the case may be.../Whatever it is.../Be that as it may...

Fuera lo que fuese = Whatever the case was.../ Whatever it was...

Note: You use 'cual' with this expression when you are referring to a concrete thing like a problem, a cost, a reason. When you are referring to something unknown, you will use 'lo que'.

Here are some examples of how they are used:

Sea lo que sea, tendremos que arreglarlo tan pronto como sea posible.

Whatever the case (may be), we will have to fix it as soon as possible.

Sea cual sea su problema, no podemos aceptar que siga portándose mal.

Whatever his problem may be we can't accept him continuing to behave badly.

Fuera cual fuese su razonamiento, el plan no le salió nada bien.

Whatever his reasoning was, the plan didn't work out well for him at all.

Fuera lo que fuese, causó un impacto muy positivo.

Whatever it was, it caused a very positive impact.

How does that sit with you? Have you got the idea?

Great!

Vayas adonde/donde vayas...

This one translates as, 'No matter where you go... and is used in this way:

Vayas adonde vayas, nunca vas a encontrar a nadie como él.

No matter where you go you'll never find someone like him.

Vayas donde vayas, el mundo seguirá siendo igual.

No matter where you go, the world will continue to be the same.

Digas lo que digas...

Perhaps you are starting to second guess the meanings of these expressions now. This one translates as something like: No matter what you say... And is used this way:

Digas lo que digas, no me vas a convencer.

Whatever you say, you're not going to convince me.

Diga lo que diga él, yo sé la verdad.

Whatever he says, I know the truth.

Note: Interestingly, this kind of structure can be used with any structure that is saying: 'Whatever the...'

e.g.

Cueste lo que cueste. = Whatever it costs.

...lo que me dé la gana.

There are various versions of this expression, some of which are a little risqué. However, this one tends to be the most common and one that you can use in mixed company.

It translates a something like: whatever I fancy/want.

This is how it is used:

Diga lo que me diga ella, yo voy a hacer lo que me dé la gana.

No matter what she tells me, I'm going to do whatever I fancy/want.

Una vez allí puedes hacer lo que te dé la gana.

Once you're there you can do whatever you fancy.

Bueno, bueno, bueno, this brings us to the end of our 'weird and wonderful' part of the subjunctive. Now, let's practise a little, using the expressions that we have been looking at.

Ahora tú.

Exercise 38

1, No matter how funny he is, I'm not going to the show.

_____

2, No matter where they go, they'll always find a way to earn a living.

_____

_____

3, Pedro doesn't care what they say to him, he is going to do what he fancies.

_____

_____

4, If you dare to tell me you're not here tomorrow you'll have problems. (tú)

_____

5, We'll spend time with them as long as they behave properly.

_____

6, As far as I know the mayor hasn't been here for a week.

_____

7, Be that as it may, I'm not in agreement.

_____

8, I don't mind, whatever you say. (usted)

_____

9, Tell him that we can go there or he can come here. As he wishes. (tú)

_____

_____

10, Whatever it was that caused the explosion , we all have had quite a shock.

_____

_____

Time out to contemplate.

Well, would you believe it if we told you that you have now finished the book?...erm, well, not quite. We still have one more thing to do and that is to complete each and every exercise again. Fortunately, this is the last time you will be working through them!

By the time you've finished them you should be more than ready to use the subjunctive with confidence and ability. Of course, you don't need to go all out to force it into your conversations. Rather, you may well find that it just naturally, organically starts to spill out into your day to day interactions.

You'll probably find that you will begin to notice it more and more in the texts that you read. You'll hear it on all sides as you begin to notice the triggers standing out from the rest of the sounds.

If reaching this part of the book proves one thing, it proves that you have the skill and the determination to really master the subjunctive and we just want to take a moment to congratulate you. As we have mentioned, you can now put yourself amongst the very few non-native speakers of the Spanish language who understand and can use the subjunctive well. This is no small feat and you can be very proud of that achievement.

Does this mean you'll always use it correctly? No! Does this mean that you will never be confused again? No! That's normal. It's going to happen.

What it does mean, however, is that you now have a fantastic framework on which you can hang your Spanish and your understandings as well as having something on which you can build going forward.

Cynthia y yo esperamos que te haya gustado este libro y esta experiencia y que sigas aprendiendo y mejorando tu español.

Vayas donde vayas en los países de habla hispana, el subjuntivo se usará todos los días en cada momento. Y, nos alegramos de que estés preparado/a para usarlo como si formara parte de tu lengua materna.

No queremos decir que ésta sea la única cosa importante que aprender del español, pero qué fenomenal que ya lo domines.

Es importante que repases con frecuencia este libro y queremos que hagas de nuevo todos los ejercicios.

Fuera cual fuese tu nivel antes de empezar este libro, es muy posible que ahora hayas alcanzado otro nivel mucho más impresionante.

Now, let's get going on the last round of exercises. Pay special attention to how much more accurate and confident you are this time around. Oh, and watch how quickly you go through everything too.

Ahora te toca a ti....por última vez.

Exercise 21

1, Unless they tell you, you can always ask them to give you an extra day. (tú)

_____

_____

2, After we arrive do you want us to do anything in particular? (usted)

_____

_____

3, How frustrating that they don't want us to be there tomorrow. *

_____

4, It's ridiculous that we pay so many taxes when all we need is that they provide the basic services.

_____

_____

5, The fascinating thing is that we can choose whatever we like.

_____

_____

Exercise 14a

1, The boss doesn't have any job that I can do right now.

_____

2, Is there a phone around here where I can make a call?

_____

3, Do they know anyone who works with animals?

_____

4, Do you have anything that I can make to eat? (usted)

_____

5, I'm looking for a secretary who has a lot of flexibility.

_____

6, There's nothing you can drink here. (tú)

_____

7, Do we have anything that we can give them?

_____

8, The ice-cream seller doesn't have anything that you want. (ustedes)

_____

9, Is there somewhere I can get a shower?

_____

10, Do you know anyone who makes made to measure clothing.

_____

Exercise 11

1, It's impossible that they know what is happening. (saber)

_____

2, It's doubtful that I can do that for next week. (hacer)

_____

3, It's probable that we will be there on Monday. (estar)*

_____

4, It's likely that you will have problems. (tener) (usted)*

_____

5, It's possible that they'll tell me in the morning. (decírmelo)

6, It's not true that he wants to see it.

7, It's uncertain that the dentist can see you right away.

8, It's unlikely that we'll win the lottery.

Exercise 6b

1, The usual thing is that my friends organise a party for me. (organizar)

2, The worst thing is that I don't know what's going on. (saber/pasar)

3, The fascinating thing about all the problems that they have is that they don't do more. (hacer)

4, The logical thing is that they come here first. (venir)

_____

5, The frustrating thing is that nobody thinks about me. (pensar en mí)

_____

Exercise 32

1, If I could, I would buy you a diamond ring.(usted)

_____

2, If you had a million Euros, what would you do?(tú)

_____

3, If they spoke to the man responsible, do you think he would admit to it? (tú)

_____

_____

4, If your girlfriend pays for the ticket, will she go?(tú)

_____

5, If you paid would she go? (ustedes)

_____

6. If I were you, I would tell him as soon as possible. (vosotros/ustedes)

_____

7, If it comes today, where will you put the vase? (tú)

_____

8, If we leave this afternoon, we'll be there by tomorrow.

_____

9, If the doctor told you that, then you would have to do it. (usted)

_____

10, If the doctor tells you that, will you do it? (tú)

_____

Exercise 6a

Let's practice these Opinion triggers by translating the following sentences into Spanish:

1, It fascinates me that my teacher comes to school on roller boots. (venir/patines)

_____

_____

2, It's annoying that the politicians never answer a question. (contestar)

_____

3, Francisco likes it that his mum prepares spaghetti on Fridays. (preparar/espagueti)

_____

4, It bothers Julia that she can never find her keys. (poder/encontrar)

_____

5, The parents love it that their children come to visit them every week. (venir/visitar)

_____

6, It all depends on how we see it.

_____

7, It all depends on what they do afterwards.

_____

8, I'm scared that the connection will be terrible.

_____

9, I'm happy that my son can draw so well.

_____

Exercise 28

1, It's probable that the ship sank in that area.

_____

2, The surgeon didn't believe that the patient had a serious problem.

_____

3, I very much doubt that the grandchildren did that on purpose.

_____

4, The stranger wanted to know if there was anyone who was able to help him.

_____

5, So, didn't you have anything that was strong enough to hold it? (ustedes)

_____

6, The president wasn't saying that he was going to fix the problems easily.

_____

7, There was nothing we could do that would make him happy again.

_____

8, Maybe the prime minister knew something that we didn't.

9, The identical twins deny that they were involved.

10, At that moment I didn't know anyone who spoke Spanish.

Exercise 8

1, I suggest that you drink it in one go. (beberlo de golpe) (vosotros/ustedes)

2, He recommends that we don't say anything for the moment. (no decir nada de momento)

3, So, you want me to call, do you? (llamar) (usted)

4, I prefer you not to do that here. (hacer) (tú)

5, It's advisable that they only read the first two pages. (leer páginas)

_____

6, I don't want you to come with me tomorrow. (venir conmigo)

_____

7, He wants to stay here. (quedarse)

_____

8, My father prohibits us to go out after nine.

_____

9, I advise you to study this book every day. (estudiar)

_____

10, We recommend that you frequently listen to Spanish. (escuchar frecuentemente) (Do all the 'you' versions)

_____

_____

_____

_____

Exercise 6c.

1, It's fabulous that they want to help us. (fabuloso)

_____

2, How sad that she can't come for the wedding. (triste)

_____

3, It's curious that you work so well under pressure.
(curioso/bajo presión)

_____

4, How strange, and I don't mean that in a funny way, that
I'm eating so much chocolate this week. (raro)

_____

5, It's incredible that there are so many wars in the world.
(increíble/guerras)

_____

6, How worrying that they aren't here yet. (preocupante)

_____

7, It's funny that they don't talk to one another anymore.
(gracioso/ya no se hablan)

_____

_____

8, That they don't come here is very strange. (mixed up, but still a trigger)

_____

9, From my point of view it's terrible that we don't see them these days. (terrible)

_____

10, How frustrating that we can't go there tomorrow. (frustrante)

_____

11, The worst thing is that they don't want to say anything. (decir nada)

_____

12, The logical thing is that you get here for eight tomorrow morning. (llegar para)

_____

Exercise 17

1, I'm taking an umbrella in case it rains. (llover)

_____

2, We are going to eat at three unless you are hungry now. (tú)

_____

3, The guys are going to the bar after they eat.

_____

4, Don't leave without paying. (Usted.)

_____

5, The girls are waiting until we get there.

_____

6, I'll do it as long as it makes you happy.(tú)

_____

7, Whilst you are here can you fix that light? (Usted.)

_____

8, So that it works, we have to fill the machine with water. (funcionar)

_____

9, Give me that before it breaks. (romperse) (tú)

_____

10, Once we tell them, we can do it.

_____

11, You can have whatever you want at the party.

_____

12, Even if she comes here to ask me directly, I won't do it.

_____

Exercise 25

1, The pilot hoped that the passengers were calm during the whole journey.

_____

2, Ana and Alfonso expected that their parents would say something to them about their behaviour.

_____

3, The nun hoped that the priest would allow her to write the next sermon.

_____

4, Alejandro waited for twenty minutes for his teacher to come and talk to him.

_____

5, Cynthia was expecting her exam results to be good.

_____

Exercise 34

1, I wish the girl in the next office would talk to me.

_____

2 , If only the bank manager had given him the loan.

_____

3, If only my students would study a little bit harder.

_____

4, If only my teacher had taught me how to do it properly.

_____

5, I wish I could see my grandmother just one more time.

_____

6, If only there were more people like you in the world. (tú)

_____

7, If only the lights would work on the car.

_____

8, I wish the show had gone on forever.

_____

9, If only we could talk more by Skype.

_____

10, I wish that Juana had told me how she felt before leaving.

_____

Exercise 6

1, It's incredible that the runners can cover so much distance. (poder cubrir)

_____

2, It's not good that we all think that. (pensar)

_____

3, It's curious that they never look at me. (mirar)

_____

4, How strange that it isn't where I left it. (estar/dejar)

_____

5, How awesome that you're here with me.

_____

Exercise 15

1, When we eat in my family's house, we often have chicken.

_____

2, When we eat in my family's house tomorrow, we will have chicken.

_____

3, When we go on holiday we'll take lots of sun-cream.

_____

4, When we go on holiday we take lots of sun cream.

_____

5, When you drive on Saturday, take care.

_____

6, When you drive you normally take care.

_____

7, When they talk to me they smile.

_____

8, When they talk to me they'll smile.

_____

9, When we are in Spain, we'll visit the beach.

_____

10, When we are in Spain, we visit the beach.

_____

Exercise 35

1, Don't talk to me as if I were an idiot! (tú)

_____

2, I'd like you to work as if you were the owner of the business. (usted)

_____

3, Marco arrived tired as if he had had a long day.

_____

4, You are talking as if the world was about to end. (vosotros/ustedes)

_____

5, It's as if it never happened.

_____

Exercise 18

1, As soon as the builder gives us a date we can make a plan.

_____

2, Once my father falls asleep I'll call you. (dormirse) (tú)

_____

3, As soon as I know more, I'll tell you. (ustedes)

_____

4, Once the president signs, it's all over. (acabarse todo)

_____

5, As soon as we sit down you can begin to serve the food. (ustedes)

_____

Exercise 30

1, We hoped that our friends would tell us about the birth as soon as they knew.

_____

_____

2, It was curious that Juan, the neighbour's son who goes to the same school as my son, didn't arrive on time yesterday.

_____

_____

3, I used to believe that it wasn't possible that they could do such terrible things.

_____

_____

4, I thought the girls weren't coming until three.

_____

5, I didn't know if the neighbours knew that we were moving to Spain.

_____

_____

6, Pedro and María hoped that the train wouldn't arrive before they bought their tickets.

7, I didn't doubt that the man was telling the truth but I wasn't sure that he knew the whole story.

8, Guillermo thinks that his brother didn't want him to go with him so that he could do something naughty.

9, Maribel wasn't saying that she needed her things by the next day, but that it was important that she had them that week.

10, José María didn't like that Ernesto, whose daughter was dating his son, was telling them what they could and couldn't do.

Exercise 10

1, I want you to stop doing that. (dejar de) (usted)

2, If only they would decide. (decidir)

3, It's better that you don't listen to that. (escuchar) (tú)

4, I'm begging you to see my point of view. (ver mi punto de vista) (ustedes)

5, I hope I pass the exam. (aprobar)

6, It's not important that you start at eight in the morning. (empezar) (vosotros/ustedes)

7, It's curious that she wants to wait a few months. (esperar)

8, They hope that the police arrive quickly. (llegar)

_____

9, It's vital that you read the entire letter. (leer) (ustedes)

_____

10, I prefer that they don't get up until later. (levantarse)

_____

Exercise 22.

1, It's advisable that the head teacher prohibits that the students use mobiles in the classroom.

_____

_____

2, How terrible that the partners are saying that the investors must withdraw their money.

_____

_____

3, As long as it is important that we know that information, we should learn it well.

_____

_____

Exercise 5

1, We hope that we hear something soon. (oír algo pronto)

2, They hope that the others arrive on time. (llegar a tiempo)

3, I hope to go to university next year. (ir a la universidad)

4, She hopes that he asks the question. (hacer la pregunta)

5, She hopes to be president of the club. (ser presidente)

Exercise 26

1, It's good that Cristina caught her flight.

2, How awesome that Pedro passed his exams.

3, It used to fascinate me that the neighbour never left his house during the day.

4, It annoyed me that I had to wait half an hour alone in his office.

5, It's incredible that I really met Manu Chao.

6, How nice that your boyfriend bought you that for your birthday. (tú)

7, It bothered him that it rained without pause that week.

8, My dad loved it that I was able to get a job in his firm.

9, How frustrating that nobody knew where the wedding was.

10, It's better that it happened like that.

Exercise 36

1, Shut up I'm talking. (tú)

2, Come tomorrow, I'll be there. (usted)

_____

3, Eat the food, if not you'll be hungry later.
(vosotros/ustedes)

_____

4, Don't talk to me like that, you don't have the right. (tú)

_____

5, Be still a moment, I'm trying to put your clothes on. (tú)

_____

Exercise 33a

1, It could be possible that I'm learning this well.

_____

2, I'd like it to be true.

_____

3, Would you want me to do that now. (tú)

_____

4, For there to be a better atmosphere we would need to
talk.

_____

5, I wouldn't want you to feel bad about what happened. (Usted)

Exercise 19

1, We can't go until they give us the keys.

2, As long as the doctor signs me off today, I'll be at work tomorrow. (Dar el alta.)

3, I always drink water when I eat.

4, I'll call you as soon as my friends go. (tú)

5, I can't help you unless you tell me what's wrong.

6, Here, take this money with you in case you have to buy something. (ustedes)

7, At least have a coffee while you're here with me. (tú)

8, As soon as I retire I'm off to Mexico. (jubilarse)

9, What do you do that for? So that the food has a nice flavour. (tú)

_____

10, Without knowing it, you are saying exactly what I think. (usted)

_____

11, We must get bread before we go back home.

_____

12, When I eat today, I'm going to have a big steak.

_____

13, I'll have whatever there is.

_____

14, Whatever! (ser) (They say, whatever it may be.)

_____

15, As soon as I get into my car I put on my seat belt.

_____

Exercise 18a

1, As soon as the police arrive we'll tell them everything.

_____

2, As soon as they arrive we go straight to the garden.

_____

3, As soon as we get the ball we run as fast as possible.

_____

4, As soon as we get the ball we'll attack.

_____

5, As soon as the priest arrives, we'll sit down.

_____

Exercise 9

1, It's better that they talk amongst themselves. (hablar entre sí)

_____

2, There's no need for us to finish the work today. (terminar)

_____

3, I insist that they tell me everything. (decir/contar)

_____

4, It's better for you to take it easy. (tomarlo con calma) (tú)

_____

5, There's no need for you to take that attitude. (tomar esa actitud) (ustedes)

_____

6, The mayor insists that the people keep calm. (el alcalde, mantener la calma)

_____

7, Seeing her makes me think of my sister.

_____

8, The teacher often lets the children leave early.

_____

Exercise 27

1, The landlord always preferred that I paid the rent at the end of the month.

_____

2, The shop assistant asked me to show her my identification.

_____

3, It was important that Mercedes took her tablets each hour.

_____

4, It was preferable that the guests didn't go into that room.

_____

5, There was no need for your mother to say that to you. (tú)

6, The captain insisted that his team ate a light lunch before the game.

7, The waiter recommended that we tried the Spanish omelette.

8, It was advisable that everyone took a coat with them.

9, The people there suggested that we caught the next bus to Madrid.

10, It was unnecessary for so many people to die during the First World War.

Exercise 20

1, The dog likes its owners to spend time with him, walk him every day and give him good food.

2, María thinks that it is strange that her boyfriend doesn't call and doesn't visit her as much as before.

_____

_____

3, As soon as I finish painting and making the dinner, I'll go to pick you up. (tú)

_____

_____

4, It's possible that the boys are in their class now and can't answer their phones.

_____

_____

Exercise 7.

1, It's advisable that she be there for the meeting. (estar para)

_____

2, It's vital that we give him the information. (darle la información)

_____

3, It's necessary that he talk with the doctor soon. (hablar con)

_____

4, It's not important that they know that. (saber eso)

_____

5, It's not necessary that I go with them. (ir/irse)

_____

Exercise 38

1, No matter how funny he is, I'm not going to the show.

_____

2, No matter where they go, they'll always find a way to earn a living.

_____

3, Pedro doesn't care what they say to him, he is going to do what he fancies.

_____

4, If you dare to tell me you're not here tomorrow you'll have problems. (tú)

_____

5, We'll spend time with them as long as they behave properly.

_____

6, As far as I know the mayor hasn't been here for a week.

_____

7, Be that as it may, I'm not in agreement.

_____

8, I don't mind, whatever you say. (usted)

_____

9, Tell him that we can go there or he can come here. As he wishes. (tú)

_____

_____

10, Whatever it was that caused the explosion , we all have had quite a shock.

_____

_____

Exercise 31

1, How interesting that the team had known that all of the time.

_____

2, The photographer hoped that his photos had come out well.

_____

3, We were all going to stay out until we found the ball.

_____

4, I didn't doubt that Ricardo had done a fabulous job.

_____

5, We all agreed that when we had finished painting we would go to the bar.

_____

6, The nurse didn't want to say anything in case someone had already told her

_____

7, It was good that Pedro had organised his own party.

_____

8, It was interesting that no one had realised the time.

_____

9, It's doubtful that anyone had know about the problems beforehand.

10, It's not true that the neighbour had been here earlier that day.

Exercise 14

1, The man denies that he forgets a lot. (olvidarse)

2, The town hall insist that the lights go out at eleven. (apagarse)

3, It's probable that nobody will arrive until after ten. (llegar)

4, It's advisable that everyone wears a lifejacket. (llevar/un chaleco salvavidas)

5, The teacher orders that all the children be quiet. (callarse)

6, I beg you not to talk with him again. (hablar con/tú)

_____

7, The logical thing is that you buy this car right now. (comprar/tú)

_____

8, It's fantastic that both the men are talking to one another now. (hablarse)

_____

9, It fascinates him that his children know so much. (saber)

_____

10, It's annoying that we pay so many taxes. (pagar impuestos)

_____

11, It interests me that you think that. (pensar/tú)

_____

12, If only she would pay attention to me. (prestar atención)

_____

13, We love it that our friends are so interesting.

_____

14, There's no need for you to say anything. (decir/usted)

_____

15, The soldiers don't believe that they are winning the war. (ganar/guerra)

_____

16, The young girl hopes to go to Spain to see a friend. (ir/se)

_____

17, Maybe I'm wrong. (estar equivocado) (It's fairly certain.)

_____

18, It's impossible that those shapes are people. (formas/ser)

_____

19, We prefer that you don't see him anymore. (verlo/ya no/tú)

_____

20, How horrible that not even you tell me the truth. (decir/ni siquiera/la verdad/usted)

_____

21, The boss doesn't doubt that his staff need a break.

_____

22, The child believes that his friends don't want to spend time with him.

_____

23, I don't deny that I am involved.

_____

24, They imagine that they won't go to Spain again.

_____

25, I don't doubt that he's a good teacher.

_____

Exercise 4.

1, I'm waiting for them to arrive.

_____

2, If only she would come today. (venir hoy)

_____

3, They hope that their children pass the exam. (aprobar el examen)

_____

4, She hopes that they make the cake today. (hacer/preparar la tarta)

_____

Exercise 12

1, My neighbour believes that I'm not going to Spain to live.

_____

2, I don't doubt that the crisis will end soon. (acabarse)

_____

3, I don't imagine that I'll get married before you. (casarse/tú)

_____

4, The fans don't deny that their team has problems. (los fanáticos)

_____

5, I suppose that the grandparents will be able to go to the show.

_____

6, My boss doesn't think that we deserve a pay rise. (merecerse/aumento de sueldo)

_____

7, Do you doubt that I'm capable of doing it? (tú)

_____

8, They just don't imagine that it can be possible.

_____

9, I'm not saying that Elizabeth can't do it.

10, We believe they can't do it and their coach doesn't believe they can do it either.

---

11. Your teacher doesn't deny that you work hard in class. (tú)

12, I'm saying that the staff do that today.

13, The fact that she lives here isn't an excuse.

14, This is a bad situation but it doesn't mean that there isn't a solution.

Exercise 33

1, If you had a friend there I didn't see her. (tú)

2, If he ate the whole pie, I didn't know anything about it.

_____

3, If they were going to send me it, it never arrived.

_____

4, If they thought they could do that then they didn't count on me.

_____

_____

5, If you gave me the keys I don't know where I put them. (tú)

_____

Exercise 13

1, Maybe my sister will be at the party on Friday. (Less likely.)

_____

2, Maybe you know better than me. (Less likely.)

_____

3, Perhaps I'll leave you in the shopping centre. (Less likely.)

_____

4, Perhaps we'll find out next week. (Enterarse) (Less likely.)

5, Maybe the machine is broken. (estar roto) (More likely.)

Exercise 29

1, Father said that as long as I got good grades, I could go skiing in Italy.

2, The man was going to work until it became dark.

3, Spain changed a lot after the Moors arrived there.

4, The chef added more cream so the food would taste better.

5, We were going to look for Elizabeth as soon as the others arrived.

Exercise 16

1, When will they arrive?

2, When they arrive will there be cake?

_____

3, When are we going to watch the movie/film?

_____

4, We will order a pizza for when we watch the film/movie.

_____

5, When will you read the book? When you are in Spain?(tú)

_____

6, I don't know when she'll arrive.

_____

7, When she arrives we can talk about the plans.

_____

8, When you get the information will you inform me please?(usted)

_____

9, I'll call you when I'm at the office.

_____

10, When will you be in the office?

_____

Note: For sake of space and so as to not repeat the exercises too closely together, we haven't included the last round in the power of three of numbers 32 to 38. Please take the time to go back and run through them again.

Exercise 23

1, How awesome that the team have won for the third time.

2, Unless Elena has written it herself, I can't accept it.

3, It interests Guillermo that all of his friends have grown beards. (dejarse crecer)

4, My parents-in-law love that they have been able to see their grandson every day.

5, The politician denies that he has been involved in the dirty business of accepting bribes.

6, Leticia doubts that her husband has remembered her birthday.

7, It's better that you have spoken with Diego before he leaves for Paris. (tú)

8, Cristina prefers that the dogs have had their walk before nine o'clock.

9, Mari Carmen says that it's important that all of the people have arrived by twelve.

10, The logical thing is that you have seen the papers before the lawyer arrives. (ustedes)

Ya has terminado de verdad...y ahora, como te prometimos, ¡puedes tomar una copa de cava con nosotros!

¡Salud !Enhorabuena! ¡Felicidades! ¡Fenomenal!

¡Buen trabajo! !Eres espectacular!

Thank you so much! ¡Muchísimas gracias!

You really have done a fantastic job. Just take in the fact that you have made it to this point and that you've actually created more than 600 sentences using the subjunctive! That level of practice is going to guarantee your success. There's no doubt about it.

Cynthia and I want to thank you for taking the time to work through this book and for supporting us in our work. LightSpeed Spanish wouldn't be anything without our supporters and we are very conscious of that when we produce tools to help you improve your Spanish.

We would really appreciate any feedback you might have and look forward to meeting you again either in our next publication, on our Facebook group or via Youtube.

Un fuerte abrazo,

Gordon y Cynthia.

Exercise 1.

BAILAR = TO DANCE

Yo	BAILE	Nosotros	BAILEMOS
Tú	BAILES	Vosotros	BAILÉIS
Él		Ellos	
Ella	BAILE	Ellas	BAILEN
Usted		Ustedes	

CONTESTAR = TO ANSWER

Yo	CONTESTE	Nosotros	CONTESTEMOS
Tú	CONTESTES	Vosotros	CONTESTÉIS
Él		Ellos	
Ella	CONTESTE	Ellas	CONTESTEN
Usted		Ustedes	

COMPRAR = TO BUY

Yo	COMPRE	Nosotros	COMPREMOS
Tú	COMPRES	Vosotros	COMPRÉIS
Él		Ellos	
Ella	COMPRE	Ellas	COMPREN
Usted		Ustedes	

Exercise 2.

BEBER = TO DRINK

Yo	BEBA	Nosotros	BEBAMOS
Tú	BEBAS	Vosotros	BEBÁIS
Él		Ellos	
Ella	BEBA	Ellas	BEBAN
Usted		Ustedes	

LEER = TO READ

Yo	LEA	Nosotros	LEAMOS
Tú	LEAS	Vosotros	LEÁIS
Él		Ellos	
Ella	LEA	Ellas	LEAN
Usted		Ustedes	

ABRIR = TO OPEN

Yo	ABRA	Nosotros	ABRAMOS
Tú	ABRAS	Vosotros	ABRÁIS
Él		Ellos	
Ella	ABRA	Ellas	ABRAN
Usted		Ustedes	

ESCRIBIR = TO WRITE

Yo	ESCRIBA	Nosotros	ESCRIBAMOS
Tú	ESCRIBAS	Vosotros	ESCRIBÁIS
Él		Ellos	
Ella	ESCRIBA	Ellas	ESCRIBAN
Usted		Ustedes	

Exercise 3.

DECIR = TO SAY

Yo	DIGA	Nosotros	DIGAMOS
Tú	DIGAS	Vosotros	DIGÁIS
Él		Ellos	
Ella	DIGA	Ellas	DIGAN
Usted		Ustedes	

SALIR = TO LEAVE/GO OUT

Yo	SALGA	Nosotros	SALGAMOS
Tú	SALGAS	Vosotros	SALGÁIS
Él		Ellos	
Ella	SALGA	Ellas	SALGAN
Usted		Ustedes	

Exercise 4.

Note: *In all the forthcoming answers you will see the personal pronouns in brackets sometimes, like this (Yo), (Tú) etc. This is to show that these could be used but don't need to be present for the sentence to be correct. Spanish speakers drop them in and out of sentences according to the need to emphasis or clear up any doubt. So, if you add them or not, as long as your verb agrees, then you are fine.*

1, (Yo) Espero a que (ellos) lleguen.

This could also be: 'Estoy esperando...' For the sake of brevity we will always use the normal present tense knowing that in some of the cases, the present continuous is also correct.

(Notice how the 'U' has to be inserted into the verb to keep the 'G' strong. This happens quite frequently, watch out for it. In this case the 'U' has no sound.)

2, Ojalá que (ella) venga hoy.

3, (Ellos) Esperan que sus niños aprueben el examen.

4, (Ella) Espera que hagan/preparen la tarta hoy.

Exercise 5

1, Esperamos oír algo pronto. (not subjunctive)

2, (Ellos) Esperan que los otros lleguen a tiempo. (subjunctive)

3, (Yo) Espero ir a la universidad el año que viene. (not subjunctive)

4, (Ella) Espera que él haga la pregunta.

5, (Ella) Espera ser presidente/a del club.

Exercise 6

1, Es increíble que los corredores puedan cubrir tanta distancia.

2, No es bueno que todos (nosotros) pensemos eso.

3, Es curioso que (ellos) nunca me miren./ ...que (ellos) no me miren nunca.

4, Qué raro que no esté dónde lo dejé.

5, Qué genial/estupendo que (tú) estés aquí conmigo.

Exercise 6a

1, Me fascina que mi profesor venga al colegio en patines.

2, Cabrea que los políticos nunca contesten a una pregunta./...no contesten nunca...

3, A Francisco le gusta que su madre prepare espaguetis los viernes.

4, A Julia le molesta que nunca pueda encontrar sus llaves./..que no pueda encontrar sus llaves nunca.

5, A los padres les encanta que sus hijos vengan a visitarlos cada semana.

6, Todo depende de cómo (nosotros) lo veamos.

7, Todo depende de lo que (ellos) hagan después.

8, Tengo miedo de que la conexión sea terrible.

9, Me alegro de que mi hijo pueda dibujar tan bien.

Exercise 6b

1, Lo habitual es que mis amigos organicen una fiesta para mí.

2, Lo peor es que (yo) no sepa qué pasa/está pasando.

3, Lo fascinante de todos los problemas que (ellos) tienen es que no hagan más.

4, Lo lógico es que (ellos) vengan aquí primero.

5, Lo frustrante es que nadie piense en mí.

Exercise 6c

1, Es fabuloso que (ellos) quieran ayudarnos

2, Qué triste que (ella) no pueda venir para la boda.

3, Es curioso que (tú) trabajes tan bien bajo presión.

4, Qué raro, y no quiero decir eso de manera graciosa, que (yo) coma tanto chocolate esta semana.

5, Es increíble que haya tantas guerras en el mundo.

6, Qué preocupante que todavía (ellos) no estén aquí.

7, Es gracioso que (ellos) ya no se hablen.

8, Que (ellos) no vengan aquí es muy extraño/raro.

9, Desde mi punto de vista es terrible que no los veamos (a ellos) estos días.

10, Qué frustrante que (nosotros) no podamos ir allí mañana.

11, Lo peor es que (ellos) no quieran decir nada.

12, Lo lógico es que llegues para las ocho mañana por la mañana.

Exercise 7.

1, Es aconsejable que (ella) esté allí para la reunión/junta.

2, Es vital/imprescindible que le demos(a él) la información.

3, Es necesario/preciso que (él) hable con el médico pronto.

4, No es importante que (ellos) sepan eso.

5, No es necesario que (me) vaya con ellos.

Exercise 8

1, (Yo) sugiero que (vosotros/ustedes) lo bebáis/beban de una vez/de golpe.

2, (Él) (nos) recomienda que no digamos nada de/por el momento.

3, Así que, (usted) quiere que yo llame, ¿verdad/no?

4, (Yo) prefiero que no hagas eso aquí.

5, Conviene que (ellos) sólo lean las primeras dos páginas.

6, (Yo) no quiero que (tú) vengas conmigo mañana.

7, (Él) quiere quedarse aquí. (Did you remember the rule?)

8, Mi padre (nos) prohíbe que (nosotros) salgamos después de las nueve.

9, (Yo) te aconsejo que (tú) estudies este libro cada día.

10, (Nosotros) (te) recomendamos que (tú) escuches el español frecuentemente.

Or: (Nosotros) (os) recomendamos que (vosotros) escuchéis el español frecuentemente.

Or: (Nosotros) (le) recomendamos que (usted) escuche el español frecuentemente.

Or: (Nosotros) (les) recomendamos que (ustedes) escuchen el español frecuentemente.

Exercise 9

1, Más vale que (ellos) hablen entre sí.

2, No hace falta que (nosotros) terminemos el trabajo hoy.

3, (Yo) insisto en que (ellos) me digan/cuenten todo.

4, Más vale que (tú) (te) lo tomes con calma.

5, No hace falta que (ustedes) tomen esa actitud.

6, El alcalde insiste en que la gente/el pueblo mantenga la calma.

7, Verla hace que (yo) piense en mi hermana.

8, El profesor frecuentemente deja que (los niños) salgan temprano .

Exercise 10

1, (Yo) quiero que (usted) deje de hacer eso.

2, Ojalá que (ellos) decidan.

3, Es mejor (plus all the other options) que (tú) no esuches eso.

4, (Yo) (les) ruego que vean mi punto de vista.

5, (Yo) espero aprobar el examen. (Did you remember the rule about someone wishing something for themselves?)

6, No es importante que (vosotros/ustedes) empecéis/empiecen a las ocho de la mañana.

7, Es curioso que (ella) quiera esperar unos meses.

8, (Ellos) esperan que la policía llegue rápidamente.

9, Es vital (and the others) que (ustedes) lean la carta entera.

10, (Yo) prefiero que (ellos) no se levanten hasta más tarde.

Exercise 11

1, Es imposible que (ellos) sepan lo que está pasando/pasa.

2, Es dudoso que (yo) pueda hacerlo para la próxima semana/la semana que viene.

3, Es probable que (nosotros) estemos allí el lunes.

4, Es probable que (usted) tenga problemas.

5, Es posible que (ellos) me lo digan por la mañana.

6, No es verdad que (él) quiera verlo.

7, Es incierto que el dentista te pueda ver enseguida/inmediatamente.

8, Es improbable que (nosotros) ganemos la lotería.

Just out of interest, often in Spain, they don't say, "I win the lottery" rather, they say, "The lottery touches me" using the verb Tocar. So, a Spanish person would probably say the above sentence this way:

'Es improbable que me toque la lotería.' = It's unlikely that the lottery will touch me.

Exercise 12

1, Mi vecino cree que no (me) voy a España a vivir. (Did you spot the non-trigger?)

2, No dudo que la crisis se acabe pronto.

3, (Yo) no me imagino que me case antes que tú.

4, Los fanáticos no niegan que su equipo esté en/tenga problemas.

5, (Yo) supongo que los abuelos pueden ir al espectáculo.

6, Mi jefe no piensa que (nosotros) nos merezcamos un aumento de sueldo.

7, ¿Dudas (tú) que (yo) sea capaz de hacerlo?

8, (Ellos) simplemente no se imaginan que pueda ser posible.

9, No digo que Elizabeth no pueda hacerlo.

10, (Nosotros) creemos que (ellos) no pueden hacerlo y su entrenador no cree que puedan hacerlo tampoco. (Did you catch the trigger and non-trigger saying the same thing?)

11, Tu profesor no niega que trabajes duramente en clase.

12, (Yo) Estoy diciendo/digo que el personal haga eso hoy.

13, El hecho de que (ella) viva aquí no es una excusa.

14, Ésta es una situación mala pero no significa que no haya una solución.

Exercise 13

1, Quizá/tal vez mi hermana esté en la fiesta el viernes.

2, Quizás/tal vez lo sepas mejor que yo.

3, Quizá te deje en el centro comercial.

4, Quizá/tal vez nos enteremos la semana que viene.

5, Tal vez/quizás la máquina está rota.

Exercise 14

1, El hombre niega que olvide mucho.

2, El ayuntamiento insiste en que las luces se apaguen a las once.

3, Es probable que no llegue nadie hasta después de las diez.

4, Es aconsejable/se aconseja que todo el mundo lleve un chaleco salvavidas.

5, El profesor manda que todos los niños se callen.

6, Te ruego que (tú) no hables con él más / de nuevo.

7, Lo lógico es que (tú) compres este coche ahora mismo.

8, Es fantástico que los dos hombres ya se hablen/se hablen ahora.

9, Le fascina que sus hijos sepan tanto.

10, Cabrea que (nosotros) paguemos tantos impuestos.

11, Me interesa que (tú) pienses eso.

12, Ojalá que (ella) me preste atención.

13, Nos encanta que nuestros amigos sean tan interesantes.

14, No hace falta que (tú) digas nada.

15, Los soldados no creen que estén ganando/ganen la guerra.

16, La chica joven espera irse a España a ver a un amigo. (Did you remember the rule about wishing for something for yourself and Esperar?)

17, Quizá/s (yo) estoy equivocado. (Did you remember the rule with Quizá/s when something is more certain?)

18, Es imposible que esas formas sean personas.

19, (Nosotros) preferimos que ya no lo veas más.

20, Qué horrible que ni siquiera usted pueda decirme la verdad.

21, El jefe no duda que su personal necesite un descanso.

22, El niño cree que sus amigos no quieren pasar tiempo con él.

23, No niego que (yo) esté involucrado.

24, (Ellos) se imaginan que no se van a España otra vez/de nuevo.

25, (Yo) no dudo que sea un buen profesor.

Exercise 14a

1, El jefe no tiene ningún trabajo que (yo) pueda hacer ahora mismo.

2, ¿Hay un teléfono por aquí desde dónde (yo) pueda hacer una llamada?

3, ¿Conocen a alguien que trabaje con animales (ellos)?

4, ¿(Usted) tiene algo que pueda hacerme de comer?

5, Busco una secretaria que tenga mucha flexibilidad.

6, No hay nada aquí que (tú) puedas beber.

7, ¿(Nosotros) tenemos alguna cosa que les podamos dar?

8, El vendedor de helados no tiene nada que (ustedes) quieran.

9, ¿Hay algún lugar en el que (yo) pueda ducharme?

10, ¿Conoces a alguien que haga ropa hecha a medida?

Exercise 15

1, Cuando (nosotros) comemos en la casa de mi familia solemos comer pollo.

2, Cuando (nosotros) comamos en la casa de mi familia mañana, comeremos pollo.

3, Cuando (nosotros, nos) vayamos de vacaciones llevaremos mucha crema solar.

4, Cuando (nosotros, nos) vamos de vacaciones llevamos mucha crema solar.

5, Cuando (tú) conduzcas el sábado, ten cuidado.

6, Cuando (tú) conduces sueles tener/normalmente tienes cuidado.

7, Cuando (ellos) me hablan, sonríen.

8, Cuando (ellos) me hablen, sonreirán.

9, Cuando (nosotros) estemos en España, visitaremos la playa.

10, Cuando (nosotros) estamos en España, visitamos la playa.

Exercise 16

1, ¿Cuándo llegarán (ellos)?

2, Cuando (ellos) lleguen ¿habrá tarta/pastel?

3, ¿Cuándo vamos a ver la película?

4, (Nosotros) pediremos pizza cuando veamos/miremos la película.

5, ¿Cuándo leerás el libro (tú)? ¿Cuando estés en España?

6, No sé cuándo llegará (ella).

7, Cuando llegue (ella), (nosotros) podemos hablar de los planes.

8, Cuando (usted) tenga/reciba la información, ¿me informará, por favor?

9, (Yo) te llamaré cuando esté en la oficina/despacho.

10, ¿Cuándo estará en la oficina/despacho (usted)?

Exercise 17

1, Me llevo un paraguas en caso de que llueva.

2, (Nosotros) vamos a comer a las tres a no ser que/a menos que (tú) tengas hambre ahora.

3, Los chicos van al bar después de que (ellos) coman. (It's also possible, and more common to say: Después de comer.)

4, No se vaya (usted) sin que pague /sin pagar. ('Sin pagar' is much more common and it is rare to hear the subjunctive version.)

5, Las chicas esperan/están esperando hasta que (nosotros) lleguemos.

6, (Yo) lo haré con tal de que te haga feliz.

7, Mientras que (usted) esté aquí ¿puede reparar/arreglar la luz?

8, Para que funcione, tenemos que llenar la máquina con/de agua.

9, Dame eso antes de que se rompa.

10, Una vez que (nosotros) se lo digamos (a ellos), podemos hacerlo.

11, (Tú) puedes tener lo que quieras en la fiesta.

12, Aunque (ella) venga a pedírmelo directamente, (yo) no lo haré.

Exercise 18

1, En cuanto/tan pronto como el constructor/el albañil nos dé una fecha (nosotros) podemos hacer/formular un plan.

2, En cuanto/tan pronto como se duerma mi padre, te llamaré.

3, Tan pronto como/en cuanto (yo) sepa más, se lo diré (a ustedes).

4, En cuanto firme el presidente, se acaba todo.

5, En cuanto/tan pronto como (nosotros) nos sentemos (ustedes) pueden empezar a servir la comida.

Exercise 18a

1, Tan pronto como/en cuanto llegué la policía se lo diremos/contaremos todo.

2, Tan pronto como/en cuanto (ellos) llegan, (nosotros) vamos directamente al jardín.

3, Tan pronto como/en cuanto cogemos/conseguimos la pelota (nosotros), corremos tan rápido como es posible.

4, Tan pronto como/en cuanto cojamos/consigamos la pelota (nosotros), atacaremos.

5, Tan pronto como/en cuanto llegue el cura, nos sentaremos.

Exercise 19

1, (Nosotros) no (nos) podemos ir hasta que (ellos) <u>no</u> nos den las llaves. (The 'no' in this answer may seem strange. It's a curiosity of this kind of sentence. They say, '...until they don't give us the keys.')

2, Con tal de que el médico/doctor me dé el alta hoy, estaré en el trabajo mañana.

3, Siempre (yo) bebo agua cuando como. (Did you remember the difference?)

4, (Yo) te llamaré en cuanto/tan pronto como (se) vayan mis amigos.

5, (Yo) no te puedo ayudar a menos que/a no ser que me digas lo que/qué pasa.

6, Tengan este dinero en caso de que (ustedes) tengan que comprar algo.

7, Por lo menos toma/tómate un café mientras que estés aquí conmigo.

8, Tan pronto como/en cuanto (yo) me jubile (me) voy a México.

9, ¿Para qué haces eso (tú)? Para que la comida tenga un buen sabor.

10, Sin que (usted) lo sepa, está diciendo/dice exactamente lo que (yo) pienso.

11, (Nosotros) debemos comprar pan antes de que volvamos a casa/ antes de volver a casa.

12, Cuando (yo) coma hoy, voy a tomar(me) un filete/bistec grande.

13, (Yo) tendré lo que haya.

14, ¡Lo que sea!

15, Tan pronto como/en cuanto me meto/entro en el coche/carro me pongo el cinturón de seguridad. (Repetitive event with 'cuando')

Exercise 20

1, Al perro le gusta que sus dueños pasen tiempo con él, que lo paseen cada día y que le den buena comida.

2, María piensa/cree que es raro que su novio no llame y que no la visite tanto como antes.

3, Tan pronto como/ en cuanto termine de pintar y prepare la cena iré a recogerte.

4, Es posible que los chicos estén en su clase ahora y que (ellos) no puedan contestar a sus móviles.

Exercise 21

1, A no ser que (ellos) te lo digan, siempre puedes pedirles que te den un día extra.

2, Después de que (nosotros) lleguemos, ¿quiere que hagamos algo en particular?

3, Qué frustrante que (ellos) no quieran que (nosotros) estemos allí mañana.

4, Es ridículo que (nosotros) paguemos tantos impuestos cuando todo lo que necesitamos es que (ellos) nos provean los servicios básicos.

5, Lo fascinante es que (nosotros) podamos elegir/escoger lo que queramos.

Exercise 22

1, Es aconsejable que el director prohíba que los estudiantes usen sus móviles/celulares en el aula.

2, Qué terrible que los socios digan que los inversores deban retirar su dinero.

3, Mientras que sea importante que (nosotros) sepamos esa información, deberíamos aprenderla bien.

Exercise 23

1, Qué asombroso que el equipo haya ganado por tercera vez.

2, A no ser que Elena lo haya escrito ella misma, no puedo aceptarlo.

3, A Guillermo le interesa que todos sus amigos se hayan dejado crecer la barba.

4, A mis suegros les encanta que hayan podido ver a su nieto cada día.

5, El político niega que haya estado involucrado en el negocio sucio de aceptar sobornos.

6, Leticia duda que su marido haya recordado/se haya acordado de su cumpleaños.

7, Es mejor que (tú) hayas hablado con Diego antes de que (él) salga para París.

8, Cristina prefiere que los perros hayan tenido su paseo antes de las nueve.

9, Mari Carmen dice que es importante que toda la gente haya llegado para las doce.

10, Lo lógico es que (ustedes) hayan visto los papeles antes de que el abogado llegue.

Exercise 24

PONER

Yo	pusiera/iese	Nosotros	pusiéramos/iésemos
Tú	pusieras/ieses	Vosotros	pusierais/ieseis
Él		Ellos	
Ella	pusiera/iese	Ellas	pusieran/iesen
Usted		Ustedes	

SABER

Yo	supiera/iese	Nosotros	supiéramos/iésemos
Tú	supieras/ieses	Vosotros	supierais/ieseis
Él		Ellos	
Ella	supiera/iese	Ellas	supieran/iesen
Usted		Ustedes	

VENIR

Yo	viniera/iese	Nosotros	viniéramos/iésemos
Tú	vinieras/ieses	Vosotros	vinierais/ieseis
Él		Ellos	
Ella	viniera/iese	Ellas	vinieran/iesen
Usted		Ustedes	

Exercise 25

1, El piloto esperaba que los pasajeros estuvieran/iesen calmados/tranquilos durante el viaje entero.

2, Ana y Alfonso esperaban que sus padres les dijeran/esen algo (a ellos) sobre su comportamiento.

3, La monja esperaba que el cura dejara/ase que (ella) escribiera el próximo sermón.

4, Alejandro esperó veinte minutos a que viniera/iese su profesor a hablar con él.

5, Cynthia esperaba que sus resultados/notas fueran/esen buenas.

Exercise 26

1, Es bueno que Cristina cogiera/tomara su vuelo.

2, Qué genial que Pedro aprobara sus exámenes.

3, Me fascinaba que el vecino nunca saliera de casa durante el día.

4, Me cabreó/enfadó/enojó que (yo) tuviera que esperar solo/a media hora en su oficina.

5, Es increíble que (yo) conociera a Manu Chao de verdad.

6, Qué bien que tu novio te comprara eso para tu cumpleaños.

7, (A él) le molestó que lloviera sin pausa esa semana.

8, A mi padre le encantó que (yo) pudiera conseguir un trabajo/empleo en su empresa.

9, Qué frustrante que nadie supiera dónde era la boda.

10, Es mejor que pasara así.

Exercise 27

1, El arrendador/casero siempre prefería que (yo) pagara el alquiler al final del mes.

2, El dependiente me pidió que le mostrara mi identificación.

3, Era importante que Mercedes tomara sus medicamentos cada hora.

4, Era preferible que los invitados no entraran en esa habitación.

5, No hacía falta que tu madre te dijera eso.

6, El capitán insistió en que su equipo comiera una comida ligera antes del partido.

7, El camarero/mesero recomendó que probáramos la tortilla española.

8, Fue aconsejable que todo el mundo se llevara un abrigo.

9, La gente allí sugirió que cogiéramos el próximo autobús a Madrid.

10, Era innecesario que tantas personas murieran durante la Primera Guerra Mundial.

Exercise 28

1, Es probable que el barco se hundiera en esa zona.

2, El cirujano no creía que el paciente tuviera un problema serio.

3, (Yo) dudo mucho que los nietos hicieran eso a propósito.

4, El extraño quiso saber si había alguien que pudiera ayudarlo.

5, Así que, (ustedes) no tenían nada que fuera suficientemente fuerte para sujetarlo.

6, El presidente no decía que fuera a arreglar todos los problemas fácilmente.

7, No había nada que (nosotros) pudiéramos hacer para hacer que estuviera/fuera feliz de nuevo.(o hacerlo feliz)

8, Tal vez el primer ministro supiera algo que no sabíamos nosotros.

9, Los gemelos niegan que estuvieran involucrados.

10, En ese momento (yo) no conocía a nadie que hablara español.

Exercise 29

1, Padre dijo que con tal de que sacara buenas notas podría ir a esquiar a Italia.

2, El hombre iba a trabajar hasta que se hiciera de noche.

3, España cambió mucho después de que llegaran los Moros. (This could also be: 'Después de llegar…')

4, El chef añadió más nata para que la comida supiera mejor.

5, (Nosotros) íbamos a buscar a Elizabeth en cuanto llegaran los otros.

Exercise 30

1, Esperábamos que nuestros amigos nos contaran sobre el parto en cuanto lo supieran.

2, Fue curioso que Juan, el hijo del vecino que va a la misma escuela que mi hijo, no llegara a tiempo ayer.

3, Solía creer/creía que no era posible que pudieran hacer cosas tan terribles.

4, (Yo) pensaba que las chicas no iban a venir hasta las tres.

5, (Yo) no sabía si los vecinos sabían que nos mudábamos a España.

6, Pedro y María esperaban que el tren no llegara antes de que compraran sus billetes/boletos.

7, (Yo) no dudaba que el hombre dijera la verdad pero no estaba seguro de que supiera la historia entera.

8, Guillermo piensa que su hermano no quiso que fuera con él para que (él) pudiera hacer algo travieso.

9, Maribel no decía que necesitara sus cosas para el día siguiente, sino que era importante que las tuviera esa semana.

10, A José María no le gustó que Ernesto, cuya hija salía con su hijo, les dijera (a ellos) lo que podían y lo que no podían hacer.

Exercise 31

1, Qué interesante que el equipo hubiera sabido eso todo el rato/tiempo.

2, El fotógrafo esperaba que sus fotos hubieran salido bien.

3, Todos íbamos a quedarnos afuera hasta que encontráramos la pelota.

4, No dudaba que Ricardo hubiera hecho un trabajo fabuloso.

5, Todos estábamos de acuerdo en que cuando hubiéramos terminado de pintar iríamos/íbamos a ir al bar.

6, La enfermera no quiso decir nada en caso de que alguien ya se lo hubiera dicho (a ella).

7, Fue bueno que Pedro hubiera organizado su propia fiesta.

8, Fue interesante que nadie se hubiera dado cuenta de la hora.

9, Es dudoso que alguien hubiera sabido de los problemas de antemano.

10, No es verdad que el vecino hubiera estado aquí más temprano ese día.

Exercise 32

1, Si (yo) pudiera le compraría (a usted) un anillo de diamantes.

2, Si tuvieras un millón de euros ¿qué harías (tú)?

3, Si (ellos) hablaran con el hombre responsable, ¿crees que lo admitiría?

4, Si paga la entrada/el billete/el boleto tu novia, ¿irá (ella)?

5, Si pagaran (ustedes), ¿iría (ella)?

6, Si yo fuera vosotros/ustedes, se lo diría tan pronto como sea/fuera posible. (Using 'sea' here makes the sentence seem more urgent. Both are fine.)

7, Si viene hoy, ¿dónde pondrás el florero?

8, Si (nosotros) salimos esta tarde estaremos allí para mañana.

9, Si el médico le dijera (a usted) eso, entonces tendría que hacerlo.

10, Si el médico te dice eso, ¿lo harás?

Exercise 33

1, Si (tú) tuviste a una amiga allí no la vi.

2, Si (él) se comió la empanada entera (yo) no supe/sabía nada de ello. (By saying 'supe' you are saying that you didn't know then. 'Sabía' means that you didn't know up until just now.)

3, Si me lo iban a enviar, nunca llegó.

4, Si (ellos) pensaban que podían hacer eso, pues no contaban conmigo.

5, Si (tú) me diste las llaves no sé dónde las puse (yo).

Exercise 33a

1, Podría ser posible que (yo) aprendiera esto bien.

2, Me gustaría que fuera la verdad.

3, ¿Querrías que hiciera eso ahora?

4, Para que hubiera un ambiente mejor necesitaríamos hablar.

5, No querría que (usted) se sintiera mal sobre lo ocurrido/lo que pasó.

Exercise 34

1, Ojalá la chica en la oficina de al lado me hablara.

2, Ojalá el director del banco le hubiera dado el préstamo.

3, Ojalá mis estudiantes estudiaran un poco más duro.

4, Ojalá mi profesor me hubiera enseñado cómo/a hacerlo bien.

5, Ojalá pudiera ver a mi abuela sólo una vez más.

6, Ojalá hubiera más gente/personas como tú en este mundo.

7, Ojalá funcionaran las luces del coche.

8, Ojalá el show/espectáculo hubiera durado para siempre.

9, Ojalá pudiéramos hablar más por Skype.

10, Ojalá Juana me hubiera dicho cómo se sentía antes de salir/irse (antes de que saliera/se fuera).

Exercise 35

1, No me hables (tú) como si (yo) fuera idiota.

2, Me gustaría que (usted) trabajara como si fuera el dueño de la empresa/el negocio.

3, Marco llegó cansado como si hubiera tenido un día largo.

4, (Vosotros/ustedes) habláis/hablan como si el mundo se fuera a acabar.

5, Es como si nunca hubiera ocurrido.

Exercise 36

1, Que te calles, estoy hablando yo.

2, Que (tú) vengas mañana, (yo) estaré allí.

3, Que (os/se) comáis/coman la comida, si no vais/van a tener hambre más tarde.

4, Que no me hables así, no tienes derecho.

5, Que te quedes quieto/te estés quieto, intento ponerte la ropa.

Exercise 37

Lo importante es que lleguemos a tiempo.

Es preciso que estemos allí a tiempo.

Es vital que nos presentemos allí a la hora prevista.

Did you have something different?

Exercise 38

1, Por muy gracioso que sea él, no voy al 'show'/espectáculo.

2, Vayan adonde/donde vayan (ellos), siempre encontrarán una manera de ganarse la vida.

3, A Pedro no le importa lo que le digan (ellos), va a hacer lo que le dé la gana. (Did you see the first trigger or did it catch you out?)

4, Como (tú) me digas que no estás aquí mañana tendrás problemas.

5, (Nosotros) pasaremos tiempo con ellos siempre y cuando se porten/se comporten bien.

6, Que yo sepa el alcalde no ha estado aquí una semana.

7, Sea lo que sea, (yo) no estoy de acuerdo/no me conformo.

8, No me importa, como diga usted.

9, Dile que podemos ir allí o él puede venir aquí. Como quiera.

10, Fuera lo que fuese lo que causó la explosión, todos hemos tenido un buen susto.

Index of Verb Conjugations.

Acabar = To end/finish/run out

yo	acabe	acabara o acabase
tú	acabes	acabaras o acabases
él, ella, Ud.	acabe	acabara o acabase
nosotros	acabemos	acabáramos o acabásemos
vosotros	acabéis	acabarais o acabaseis
ellos, ellas, Uds.	acaben	acabaran o acabasen

Apagar(se) = to switch off

yo	me apague	me apagara o me apagase
tú	te apagues	te apagaras o te apagases
él, ella, Ud.	se apague	se apagara o se apagase
nosotros	nos apaguemos	nos apagáramos o nos apagásemos
vosotros	os apaguéis	os apagarais o os apagaseis
ellos, ellas, Uds.	se apaguen	se apagaran o se apagasen

Aprobar = to pass/approve

yo	apruebe	aprobara o aprobase
tú	apruebes	aprobaras o aprobases
él, ella, Ud.	apruebe	aprobara o aprobase
nosotros	aprobemos	aprobáramos o aprobásemos
vosotros	aprobéis	aprobarais o aprobaseis
ellos, ellas, Uds.	aprueben	aprobaran o aprobasen

Beber = to drink

yo	beba	bebiera o bebiese
tú	bebas	bebieras o bebieses
él, ella, Ud.	beba	bebiera o bebiese
nosotros	bebamos	bebiéramos o bebiésemos
vosotros	bebáis	bebierais o bebieseis
ellos, ellas, Uds.	beban	bebieran o bebiesen

Callarse = to be quiet/shut up

yo	me calle	me callara o me callase
tú	te calles	te callaras o te callases
él, ella, Ud.	se calle	se callara o se callase
nosotros	nos callemos	nos calláramos o nos callásemos
vosotros	os calléis	os callarais o os callaseis
ellos, ellas, Uds.	se callen	se callaran o se callasen

Casarse = to get married

yo	me case	me casara o me casase
tú	te cases	te casaras o te casases
él, ella, Ud.	se case	se casara o se casase
nosotros	nos casemos	nos casáramos o nos casásemos
vosotros	os caséis	os casarais o os casaseis
ellos, ellas, Uds.	se casen	se casaran o se casasen

Coger = to grab/catch/take/get

yo	coja	cogiera o cogiese
tú	cojas	cogieras o cogieses
él, ella, Ud.	coja	cogiera o cogiese
nosotros	cojamos	cogiéramos o cogiésemos
vosotros	cojáis	cogierais o cogieseis
ellos, ellas, Uds.	cojan	cogieran o cogiesen

Comer = to eat

yo	coma	comiera o comiese
tú	comas	comieras o comieses
él, ella, Ud.	coma	comiera o comiese
nosotros	comamos	comiéramos o comiésemos
vosotros	comáis	comierais o comieseis
ellos, ellas, Uds.	coman	comieran o comiesen

Comprar = to buy

yo	compre	comprara o comprase
tú	compres	compraras o comprases
él, ella, Ud.	compre	comprara o comprase
nosotros	compremos	compráramos o comprásemos
vosotros	compréis	comprarais o compraseis
ellos, ellas, Uds.	compren	compraran o comprasen

Conducir = to drive

yo	conduzca	condujera o condujese
tú	conduzcas	condujeras o condujeses
él, ella, Ud.	conduzca	condujera o condujese
nosotros	conduzcamos	condujéramos o condujésemos
vosotros	conduzcáis	condujerais o condujeseis
ellos, ellas, Uds.	conduzcan	condujeran o condujesen

Conocer = to know people/places

yo	conozca	conociera o conociese
tú	conozcas	conocieras o conocieses
él, ella, Ud.	conozca	conociera o conociese
nosotros	conozcamos	conociéramos o conociésemos
vosotros	conozcáis	conocierais o conocieseis
ellos, ellas, Uds.	conozcan	conocieran o conociesen

Conseguir = to achieve/get

yo	consiga	consiguiera o consiguiese
tú	consigas	consiguieras o consiguieses
él, ella, Ud.	consiga	consiguiera o consiguiese
nosotros	consigamos	consiguiéramos o consiguiésemos
vosotros	consigáis	consiguierais o consiguieseis
ellos, ellas, Uds.	consigan	consiguieran o consiguiesen

Contar = to count

yo	cuente	contara o contase
tú	cuentes	contaras o contases
él, ella, Ud.	cuente	contara o contase
nosotros	contemos	contáramos o contásemos
vosotros	contéis	contarais o contaseis
ellos, ellas, Uds.	cuenten	contaran o contasen

Contestar = to answer

yo	conteste	contestara o contestase
tú	contestes	contestaras o contestases
él, ella, Ud.	conteste	contestara o contestase
nosotros	contestemos	contestáramos o contestásemos
vosotros	contestéis	contestarais o contestaseis
ellos, ellas, Uds.	contesten	contestaran o contestasen

Creer = to believe

yo	crea	creyera o creyese
tú	creas	creyeras o creyeses
él, ella, Ud.	crea	creyera o creyese
nosotros	creamos	creyéramos o creyésemos
vosotros	creáis	creyerais o creyeseis
ellos, ellas, Uds.	crean	creyeran o creyesen

Dar = to give

yo	dé	diera o diese
tú	des	dieras o dieses
él, ella, Ud.	dé	diera o diese
nosotros	demos	diéramos o diésemos
vosotros	deis	dierais o dieseis
ellos, ellas, Uds.	den	dieran o diesen

Deber = To must

yo	deba	debiera o debiese
tú	debas	debieras o debieses
él, ella, Ud.	deba	debiera o debiese
nosotros	debamos	debiéramos o debiésemos
vosotros	debáis	debierais o debieseis
ellos, ellas, Uds.	deban	debieran o debiesen

Decidir = To decide

yo	decida	decidiera o decidiese
tú	decidas	decidieras o decidieses
él, ella, Ud.	decida	decidiera o decidiese
nosotros	decidamos	decidiéramos o decidiésemos
vosotros	decidáis	decidierais o decidieseis
ellos, ellas, Uds.	decidan	decidieran o decidiesen

Decir = to say

yo	diga	dijera o dijese
tú	digas	dijeras o dijeses
él, ella, Ud.	diga	dijera o dijese
nosotros	digamos	dijéramos o dijésemos
vosotros	digáis	dijerais o dijeseis
ellos, ellas, Uds.	digan	dijeran o dijesen

Dejar = to leave/give up

yo	deje	dejara o dejase
tú	dejes	dejaras o dejases
él, ella, Ud.	deje	dejara o dejase
nosotros	dejemos	dejáramos o dejásemos
vosotros	dejéis	dejarais o dejaseis
ellos, ellas, Uds.	dejen	dejaran o dejasen

Dormir(se) = to (fall asleep) sleep

yo	me duerma	me durmiera o me durmiese
tú	te duermas	te durmieras o te durmieses
él, ella, Ud.	se duerma	se durmiera o se durmiese
nosotros	nos durmamos	nos durmiéramos o nos durmiésemos
vosotros	os durmáis	os durmierais o os durmieseis
ellos, ellas, Uds.	se duerman	se durmieran o se durmiesen

Empezar = to start

yo	empiece	empezara o empezase
tú	empieces	empezaras o empezases
él, ella, Ud.	empiece	empezara o empezase
nosotros	empecemos	empezáramos o empezásemos
vosotros	empecéis	empezarais o empezaseis
ellos, ellas, Uds.	empiecen	empezaran o empezasen

Encontrar = to find

yo	encuentre	encontrara o encontrase
tú	encuentres	encontraras o encontrases
él, ella, Ud.	encuentre	encontrara o encontrase
nosotros	encontremos	encontráramos o encontrásemos
vosotros	encontréis	encontrarais o encontraseis
ellos, ellas, Uds.	encuentren	encontraran o encontrasen

Enterarse = to find out/realise

yo	me entere	me enterara o me enterase
tú	te enteres	te enteraras o te enterases
él, ella, Ud.	se entere	se enterara o se enterase
nosotros	nos enteremos	nos enteráramos o nos enterásemos
vosotros	os enteréis	os enterarais o os enteraseis
ellos, ellas, Uds.	se enteren	se enteraran o se enterasen

Entrar = To enter/go in

yo	entre	entrara o entrase
tú	entres	entraras o entrases
él, ella, Ud.	entre	entrara o entrase
nosotros	entremos	entráramos o entrásemos
vosotros	entréis	entrarais o entraseis
ellos, ellas, Uds.	entren	entraran o entrasen

Escribir = to write

yo	escriba	escribiera o escribiese
tú	escribas	escribieras o escribieses
él, ella, Ud.	escriba	escribiera o escribiese
nosotros	escribamos	escribiéramos o escribiésemos
vosotros	escribáis	escribierais o escribieseis
ellos, ellas, Uds.	escriban	escribieran o escribiesen

Escuchar = to listen

yo	escuche	escuchara o escuchase
tú	escuches	escucharas o escuchases
él, ella, Ud.	escuche	escuchara o escuchase
nosotros	escuchemos	escucháramos o escuchásemos
vosotros	escuchéis	escucharais o escuchaseis
ellos, ellas, Uds.	escuchen	escucharan o escuchasen

Esperar = to wait/hope

yo	espere	esperara o esperase
tú	esperes	esperaras o esperases
él, ella, Ud.	espere	esperara o esperase
nosotros	esperemos	esperáramos o esperásemos
vosotros	esperéis	esperarais o esperaseis
ellos, ellas, Uds.	esperen	esperaran o esperasen

Estar = to be

yo	esté	estuviera o estuviese
tú	estés	estuvieras o estuvieses
él, ella, Ud.	esté	estuviera o estuviese
nosotros	estemos	estuviéramos o estuviésemos
vosotros	estéis	estuvierais o estuvieseis
ellos, ellas, Uds.	estén	estuvieran o estuviesen

Estudiar = to study

yo	estudie	estudiara o estudiase
tú	estudies	estudiaras o estudiases
él, ella, Ud.	estudie	estudiara o estudiase
nosotros	estudiemos	estudiáramos o estudiásemos
vosotros	estudiéis	estudiarais o estudiaseis
ellos, ellas, Uds.	estudien	estudiaran o estudiasen

Firmar = to sign

yo	firme	firmara o firmase
tú	firmes	firmaras o firmases
él, ella, Ud.	firme	firmara o firmase
nosotros	firmemos	firmáramos o firmásemos
vosotros	firméis	firmarais o firmaseis
ellos, ellas, Uds.	firmen	firmaran o firmasen

Funcionar = to function/work

yo	funcione	funcionara o funcionase
tú	funciones	funcionaras o funcionases
él, ella, Ud.	funcione	funcionara o funcionase
nosotros	funcionemos	funcionáramos o funcionásemos
vosotros	funcionéis	funcionarais o funcionaseis
ellos, ellas, Uds.	funcionen	funcionaran o funcionasen

Ganar = to win/earn

yo	gane	ganara o ganase
tú	ganes	ganaras o ganases
él, ella, Ud.	gane	ganara o ganase
nosotros	ganemos	ganáramos o ganásemos
vosotros	ganéis	ganarais o ganaseis
ellos, ellas, Uds.	ganen	ganaran o ganasen

Gustar = to be pleasing/to like

yo	guste	gustara o gustase
tú	gustes	gustaras o gustases
él, ella, Ud.	guste	gustara o gustase
nosotros	gustemos	gustáramos o gustásemos
vosotros	gustéis	gustarais o gustaseis
ellos, ellas, Uds.	gusten	gustaran o gustasen

Haber = to have done something

yo	haya	hubiera o hubiese
tú	hayas	hubieras o hubieses
él, ella, Ud.	haya	hubiera o hubiese
nosotros	hayamos	hubiéramos o hubiésemos
vosotros	hayáis	hubierais o hubieseis
ellos, ellas, Uds.	hayan	hubieran o hubiesen

Hablar = to talk/speak

yo	hable	hablara o hablase
tú	hables	hablaras o hablases
él, ella, Ud.	hable	hablara o hablase
nosotros	hablemos	habláramos o hablásemos
vosotros	habléis	hablarais o hablaseis
ellos, ellas, Uds.	hablen	hablaran o hablasen

Hacer = to do/make

yo	haga	hiciera o hiciese
tú	hagas	hicieras o hicieses
él, ella, Ud.	haga	hiciera o hiciese
nosotros	hagamos	hiciéramos o hiciésemos
vosotros	hagáis	hicierais o hicieseis
ellos, ellas, Uds.	hagan	hicieran o hiciesen

Hundir = to sink

yo	hunda	hundiera o hundiese
tú	hundas	hundieras o hundieses
él, ella, Ud.	hunda	hundiera o hundiese
nosotros	hundamos	hundiéramos o hundiésemos
vosotros	hundáis	hundierais o hundieseis
ellos, ellas, Uds.	hundan	hundieran o hundiesen

Imaginar = to imagine

yo	imagine	imaginara o imaginase
tú	imagines	imaginaras o imaginases
él, ella, Ud.	imagine	imaginara o imaginase
nosotros	imaginemos	imagináramos o imaginásemos
vosotros	imaginéis	imaginarais o imaginaseis
ellos, ellas, Uds.	imaginen	imaginaran o imaginasen

Ir (se) = to go away/off

yo	me vaya	me fuera o me fuese
tú	te vayas	te fueras o te fueses
él, ella, Ud.	se vaya	se fuera o se fuese
nosotros	nos vayamos	nos fuéramos o nos fuésemos
vosotros	os vayáis	os fuerais o os fueseis
ellos, ellas, Uds.	se vayan	se fueran o se fuesen

Jubilarse = to retire

yo	me jubile	me jubilara o me jubilase
tú	te jubiles	te jubilaras o te jubilases
él, ella, Ud.	se jubile	se jubilara o se jubilase
nosotros	nos jubilemos	nos jubiláramos o nos jubilásemos
vosotros	os jubiléis	os jubilarais o os jubilaseis
ellos, ellas, Uds.	se jubilen	se jubilaran o se jubilasen

Leer = to read

yo	lea	leyera o leyese
tú	leas	leyeras o leyeses
él, ella, Ud.	lea	leyera o leyese
nosotros	leamos	leyéramos o leyésemos
vosotros	leáis	leyerais o leyeseis
ellos, ellas, Uds.	lean	leyeran o leyesen

Levantarse = to get up

yo	me levante	me levantara o me levantase
tú	te levantes	te levantaras o te levantases
él, ella, Ud.	se levante	se levantara o se levantase
nosotros	nos levantemos	nos levantáramos o nos levantásemos
vosotros	os levantéis	os levantarais o os levantaseis
ellos, ellas, Uds.	se levanten	se levantaran o se levantasen

Llamar = to call

yo	llame	llamara o llamase
tú	llames	llamaras o llamases
él, ella, Ud.	llame	llamara o llamase
nosotros	llamemos	llamáramos o llamásemos
vosotros	llaméis	llamarais o llamaseis
ellos, ellas, Uds.	llamen	llamaran o llamasen

Llegar = to arrive

yo	llegue	llegara o llegase
tú	llegues	llegaras o llegases
él, ella, Ud.	llegue	llegara o llegase
nosotros	lleguemos	llegáramos o llegásemos
vosotros	lleguéis	llegarais o llegaseis
ellos, ellas, Uds.	lleguen	llegaran o llegasen

Llevar= to take/wear/carry

yo	lleve	llevara o llevase
tú	lleves	llevaras o llevases
él, ella, Ud.	lleve	llevara o llevase
nosotros	llevemos	lleváramos o llevásemos
vosotros	llevéis	llevarais o llevaseis
ellos, ellas, Uds.	lleven	llevaran o llevasen

Llover = to rain

él, ella	llueva	lloviera o lloviese

Mantener = to maintain

yo	mantenga	mantuviera o mantuviese
tú	mantengas	mantuvieras o mantuvieses
él, ella, Ud.	mantenga	mantuviera o mantuviese
nosotros	mantengamos	mantuviéramos o mantuviésemos
vosotros	mantengáis	mantuvierais o mantuvieseis
ellos, ellas, Uds.	mantengan	mantuvieran o mantuviesen

Merecerse = to deserve/to merit

yo	me merezca	me mereciera o me mereciese
tú	te merezcas	te merecieras o te merecieses
él, ella, Ud.	se merezca	se mereciera o se mereciese
nosotros	nos merezcamos	nos mereciéramos nos mereciésemos
vosotros	os merezcáis	os merecierais o os merecieseis
ellos, ellas, Uds.	se merezcan	se merecieran o se mereciesen

Mirar = to watch/look

yo	mire	mirara o mirase
tú	mires	miraras o mirases
él, ella, Ud.	mire	mirara o mirase
nosotros	miremos	miráramos o mirásemos
vosotros	miréis	mirarais o miraseis
ellos, ellas, Uds.	miren	miraran o mirasen

Morir = to die

yo	muera	muriera o muriese
tú	mueras	murieras o murieses
él, ella, Ud.	muera	muriera o muriese
nosotros	muramos	muriéramos o muriésemos
vosotros	muráis	murierais o murieseis
ellos, ellas, Uds.	mueran	murieran o muriesen

Mostrar = to show

yo	muestre	mostrara o mostrase
tú	muestres	mostraras o mostrases
él, ella, Ud.	muestre	mostrara o mostrase
nosotros	mostremos	mostráramos o mostrásemos
vosotros	mostréis	mostrarais o mostraseis
ellos, ellas, Uds.	muestren	mostraran o mostrasen

Mudarse = to move (house)

yo	me mude	me mudara o me mudase
tú	te mudes	te mudaras o te mudases
él, ella, Ud.	se mude	se mudara o se mudase
nosotros	nos mudemos	nos mudáramos o nos mudásemos
vosotros	os mudéis	os mudarais o os mudaseis
ellos, ellas, Uds.	se muden	se mudaran o se mudasen

Necesitar = to need

yo	necesite	necesitara o necesitase
tú	necesites	necesitaras o necesitases
él, ella, Ud.	necesite	necesitara o necesitase
nosotros	necesitemos	necesitáramos o necesitásemos
vosotros	necesitéis	necesitarais o necesitaseis
ellos, ellas, Uds.	necesiten	necesitaran o necesitasen

Olvidarse = to forget

yo	me olvide	me olvidara o me olvidase
tú	te olvides	te olvidaras o te olvidases
él, ella, Ud.	se olvide	se olvidara o se olvidase
nosotros	nos olvidemos	nos olvidáramos o nos olvidásemos
vosotros	os olvidéis	os olvidarais o os olvidaseis
ellos, ellas, Uds.	se olviden	se olvidaran o se olvidasen

Organizar = to organise

yo	organice	organizara u organizase
tú	organices	organizaras u organizases
él, ella, Ud.	organice	organizara u organizase
nosotros	organicemos	organizáramos u organizásemos
vosotros	organicéis	organizarais u organizaseis
ellos, ellas, Uds.	organicen	organizaran u organizasen

Pagar = to pay

yo	pague	pagara o pagase
tú	pagues	pagaras o pagases
él, ella, Ud.	pague	pagara o pagase
nosotros	paguemos	pagáramos o pagásemos
vosotros	paguéis	pagarais o pagaseis
ellos, ellas, Uds.	paguen	pagaran o pagasen

Pasar = to pass/spend(time)

yo	pase	pasara o pasase
tú	pases	pasaras o pasases
él, ella, Ud.	pase	pasara o pasase
nosotros	pasemos	pasáramos o pasásemos
vosotros	paséis	pasarais o pasaseis
ellos, ellas, Uds.	pasen	pasaran o pasasen

Pensar = to think

yo	piense	pensara o pensase
tú	pienses	pensaras o pensases
él, ella, Ud.	piense	pensara o pensase
nosotros	pensemos	pensáramos o pensásemos
vosotros	penséis	pensarais o pensaseis
ellos, ellas, Uds.	piensen	pensaran o pensasen

Poder = to be able/can

yo	pueda	pudiera o pudiese
tú	puedas	pudieras o pudieses
él, ella, Ud.	pueda	pudiera o pudiese
nosotros	podamos	pudiéramos o pudiésemos
vosotros	podáis	pudierais o pudieseis
ellos, ellas, Uds.	puedan	pudieran o pudiesen

Poner = to put

yo	ponga	pusiera o pusiese
tú	pongas	pusieras o pusieses
él, ella, Ud.	ponga	pusiera o pusiese
nosotros	pongamos	pusiéramos o pusiésemos
vosotros	pongáis	pusierais o pusieseis
ellos, ellas, Uds.	pongan	pusieran o pusiesen

Preferir = to prefer

yo	prefiera	prefiriera o prefiriese
tú	prefieras	prefirieras o prefirieses
él, ella, Ud.	prefiera	prefiriera o prefiriese
nosotros	prefiramos	prefiriéramos o prefiriésemos
vosotros	prefiráis	prefirierais o prefirieseis
ellos, ellas, Uds.	prefieran	prefirieran o prefiriesen

Preparar = to prepare

yo	prepare	preparara o preparase
tú	prepares	prepararas o preparases
él, ella, Ud.	prepare	preparara o preparase
nosotros	preparemos	preparáramos o preparásemos
vosotros	preparéis	prepararais o prepararaseis
ellos, ellas, Uds.	preparen	prepararan o preparasen

Prestar = to lend

yo	preste	prestara o prestase
tú	prestes	prestaras o prestases
él, ella, Ud.	preste	prestara o prestase
nosotros	prestemos	prestáramos o prestásemos
vosotros	prestéis	prestarais o prestaseis
ellos, ellas, Uds.	presten	prestaran o prestasen

Probar = To try/to taste

yo	pruebe	probara o probase
tú	pruebes	probaras o probases
él, ella, Ud.	pruebe	probara o probase
nosotros	probemos	probáramos o probásemos
vosotros	probéis	probarais o probaseis
ellos, ellas, Uds.	prueben	probaran o probasen

Prohibir = to prohibit

yo	prohíba	prohibiera o prohibiese
tú	prohíbas	prohibieras o prohibieses
él, ella, Ud.	prohíba	prohibiera o prohibiese
nosotros	prohibamos	prohibiéramos o prohibiésemos
vosotros	prohibáis	prohibierais o prohibieseis
ellos, ellas, Uds.	prohíban	prohibieran o prohibiesen

Proveer = to provide

yo	provea	proveyera o proveyese
tú	proveas	proveyeras o proveyeses
él, ella, Ud.	provea	proveyera o proveyese
nosotros	proveamos	proveyéramos o proveyésemos
vosotros	proveáis	proveyerais o proveyeseis
ellos, ellas, Uds.	provean	proveyeran o proveyesen

Quedarse = to remain/stay

yo	me quede	me quedara o me quedase
tú	te quedes	te quedaras o te quedases
él, ella, Ud.	se quede	se quedara o se quedase
nosotros	nos quedemos	nos quedáramos o nos quedásemos
vosotros	os quedéis	os quedarais o os quedaseis
ellos, ellas, Uds.	se queden	se quedaran o se quedasen

Querer = to want

yo	quiera	quisiera o quisiese
tú	quieras	quisieras o quisieses
él, ella, Ud.	quiera	quisiera o quisiese
nosotros	queramos	quisiéramos o quisiésemos
vosotros	queráis	quisierais o quisieseis
ellos, ellas, Uds.	quieran	quisieran o quisiesen

Recibir = to receive

yo	reciba	recibiera o recibiese
tú	recibas	recibieras o recibieses
él, ella, Ud.	reciba	recibiera o recibiese
nosotros	recibamos	recibiéramos o recibiésemos
vosotros	recibáis	recibierais o recibieseis
ellos, ellas, Uds.	reciban	recibieran o recibiesen

Romperse = to break

yo	me rompa	me rompiera o me rompiese
tú	te rompas	te rompieras o te rompieses
él, ella, Ud.	se rompa	se rompiera o se rompiese
nosotros	nos rompamos	nos rompiéramos o nos rompiésemos
vosotros	os rompáis	os rompierais o os rompieseis
ellos, ellas, Uds.	se rompan	se rompieran o se rompiesen

Saber = to know (information)

yo	sepa	supiera o supiese
tú	sepa	supieras o supieses
él, ella, Ud.	sepa	supiera o supiese
nosotros	sepamos	supiéramos o supiésemos
vosotros	sepáis	supierais o supieseis
ellos, ellas, Uds.	sepan	supieran o supiesen

Sacar = to take out/get (results)

yo	saque	sacara o sacase
tú	saques	sacaras o sacases
él, ella, Ud.	saque	sacara o sacase
nosotros	saquemos	sacáramos o sacásemos
vosotros	saquéis	sacarais o sacaseis
ellos, ellas, Uds.	saquen	sacaran o sacasen

Salir = to go out/leave

yo	salga	saliera o saliese
tú	salgas	salieras o salieses
él, ella, Ud.	salga	saliera o saliese
nosotros	salgamos	saliéramos o saliésemos
vosotros	salgáis	salierais o salieseis
ellos, ellas, Uds.	salgan	salieran o saliesen

Sentarse = to sit

yo	me siente	me sentara o me sentase
tú	te sientes	te sentaras o te sentases
él, ella, Ud.	se siente	se sentara o se sentase
nosotros	nos sentemos	nos sentáramos o nos sentásemos
vosotros	os sentéis	os sentarais o os sentaseis
ellos, ellas, Uds.	se sienten	se sentaran o se sentasen

Sentirse = to feel

yo	me sienta	me sintiera o me sintiese
tú	te sientas	te sintieras o te sintieses
él, ella, Ud.	se sienta	se sintiera o se sintiese
nosotros	nos sintamos	nos sintiéramos o nos sintiésemos
vosotros	os sintáis	os sintierais o os sintieseis
ellos, ellas, Uds.	se sientan	se sintieran o se sintiesen

Ser = to be

yo	sea	fuera o fuese
tú	seas	fueras o fueses
él, ella, Ud.	sea	fuera o fuese
nosotros	seamos	fuéramos o fuésemos
vosotros	seáis	fuerais o fueseis
ellos, ellas, Uds.	sean	fueran o fuesen

Tener = to have

yo	tenga	tuviera o tuviese
tú	tengas	tuvieras o tuvieses
él, ella, Ud.	tenga	tuviera o tuviese
nosotros	tengamos	tuviéramos o tuviésemos
vosotros	tengáis	tuvierais o tuvieseis
ellos, ellas, Uds.	tengan	tuvieran o tuviesen

Terminar = to end/finish/terminate

yo	termine	terminara o terminase
tú	termines	terminaras o terminases
él, ella, Ud.	termine	terminara o terminase
nosotros	terminemos	termináramos o terminásemos
vosotros	terminéis	terminarais o terminaseis
ellos, ellas, Uds.	terminen	terminaran o terminasen

Tocar = to touch

yo	toque	tocara o tocase
tú	toques	tocaras o tocases
él, ella, Ud.	toque	tocara o tocase
nosotros	toquemos	tocáramos o tocásemos
vosotros	toquéis	tocarais o tocaseis
ellos, ellas, Uds.	toquen	tocaran o tocasen

Tomar = to take/have/drink/eat

yo	tome	tomara o tomase
tú	tomes	tomaras o tomases
él, ella, Ud.	tome	tomara o tomase
nosotros	tomemos	tomáramos o tomásemos
vosotros	toméis	tomarais o tomaseis
ellos, ellas, Uds.	tomen	tomaran o tomasen

Trabajar = to work

yo	trabaje	trabajara o trabajase
tú	trabajes	trabajaras o trabajases
él, ella, Ud.	trabaje	trabajara o trabajase
nosotros	trabajemos	trabajáramos o trabajásemos
vosotros	trabajéis	trabajarais o trabajaseis
ellos, ellas, Uds.	trabajen	trabajaran o trabajasen

Venir = to come

yo	venga	viniera o viniese
tú	vengas	vinieras o vinieses
él, ella, Ud.	venga	viniera o viniese
nosotros	vengamos	viniéramos o viniésemos
vosotros	vengáis	vinierais o vinieseis
ellos, ellas, Uds.	vengan	vinieran o viniesen

Ver = to see/watch

yo	vea	viera o viese
tú	veas	vieras o vieses
él, ella, Ud.	vea	viera o viese
nosotros	veamos	viéramos o viésemos
vosotros	veáis	vierais o vieseis
ellos, ellas, Uds.	vean	vieran o viesen

Volver = to return/come back

yo	vuelva	volviera o volviese
tú	vuelvas	volvieras o volvieses
él, ella, Ud.	vuelva	volviera o volviese
nosotros	volvamos	volviéramos o volviésemos
vosotros	volváis	volvierais o volvieseis
ellos, ellas, Uds.	vuelvan	volvieran o volviesen

Other books published by LightSpeed Spanish:

Victor's Adventures in Spain.

A Parallel text, Audio workbook.

Available from all online book suppliers.

For more information visit:

http://www.lightspeedspanish.co.uk/victors-adventures/

Made in the USA
Lexington, KY
02 June 2018